At Issue

| Tasers

Other Books in the At Issue Series:

At Issue

I Tasers

Ronald D. Lankford Jr., Book Editor

GREENHAVEN PRESS
A part of Gale, Cengage Learning

GALE
CENGAGE Learning·

Detroit • New York • San Francisco • New Haven, Conn • Waterville, Maine • London

Elizabeth Des Chenes, *Director, Publishing Solutions*

© 2012 Greenhaven Press, a part of Gale, Cengage Learning

Gale and Greenhaven Press are registered trademarks used herein under license.

For more information, contact:
Greenhaven Press
27500 Drake Rd.
Farmington Hills, MI 48331-3535
Or you can visit our Internet site at gale.cengage.com

Articles in Greenhaven Press anthologies are often edited for length to meet page requirements. In addition, original titles of these works are changed to clearly present the main thesis and to explicitly indicate the author's opinion. Every effort is made to ensure that Greenhaven Press accurately reflects the original intent of the authors. Every effort has been made to trace the owners of copyrighted material.

LIBRARY OF CONGRESS CATALOGING-IN-PUBLICATION DATA

Tasers / Ronald D. Lankford Jr., book editor.
    p. cm. -- (At issue)
  Includes bibliographical references and index.
  ISBN 978-0-7377-5900-6 (hbk.) -- ISBN 978-0-7377-5901-3 (pbk.)
  1. Police--Equipment and supplies. 2. Stun guns. 3. Self-defense for police.
4. Nonlethal weapons. 5. Police brutality. I. Lankford, Ronald D., 1962-
  HV7936.E7T37 2011
  680--dc23
                                                                    2011053374

Printed in the United States of America
1 2 3 4 5 6 7 16 15 14 13 12

Contents

Introduction

In the span of a decade, Tasers have become an accepted crime-fighting tool. Tasers are promoted as nonlethal weapons, allowing police officers to disarm and disengage suspects without causing permanent physical harm or death. At the same time, Tasers are increasingly controversial because critics question their safety and some accuse police departments of using Tasers indiscriminately. These issues are further complicated when Tasers are deployed outside of a typical crime-fighting scenario. Whereas Tasers may provide an effective method to apprehend a criminal suspect, the weapons have been used by the police and officials at sporting events and public rallies to control unarmed audience members. Tasers are used during the course of routine traffic violations, and occasionally, have been deployed against children and elderly adults. The further Taser use moves from the frontline of crime fighting, the more controversial it becomes.

Tasers in Public Schools

On September 12, 2011, a Taser was used at a school to break up a fight between two students in Green Bay, Wisconsin. Also in September of 2011, the police used a Taser to subdue an adult suspect at Coachella Valley High School in Thermal, California. As these incidents show, Tasers have been used against both students and adults on school campuses. One reason given for Taser use at schools is safety: by having access to a Taser, a police officer has a nonlethal weapon that can protect students from harming one other while also protecting students from outside threats.

Tasers have also been used to respond to nonstudent assailants. In Colorado Springs in 2007, students reported a man in the school's parking lot who was acting suspicious. When the school's security officer investigated the situation, the suspect tried to drive away quickly and hit a tree. When the officer arrived at the car, the suspect reached toward the car's glove compartment. The police officer fired his Taser, and later learned that the assailant had a knife. In the summer of 2011, a 45-year-old man was physically assaulting his 16-year-old son on school property. When the man refused to obey the orders of police officers, a Taser was fired at him. In these scenarios, the use of a Taser helped protect students from potential danger.

In many incidences, however, the use of Tasers has been less clear cut. For example, in 2008, at Hawthorne High School in Los Angeles, a police officer fired a Taser at a 12-year-old boy. The boy had assaulted school officials and was shot with a Taser when he attempted to leave the school. While the student was breaking school rules, critics questioned the use of a Taser against the child. "This is a question of common sense. . . . You don't discharge a Taser at a child, absent the most extreme circumstances," said former federal prosecutor Michael Gennaco.[1]

In 2010, a high school sophomore was boarding a bus after school. When a police officer ordered him to pull up his baggy pants, he refused: school was over, the student said. First one officer and then another pushed the student to the ground. Each time he attempted to get up, the officers pushed him back to the ground. In the ensuing struggle, the police officers broke the student's arm and also fired a Taser into his chest.

The Future of Tasers in Schools

It may seem ironic that Tasers have created so much controversy: many police and resource officers carry other weapons, including pepper spray and handguns. In one incident in Florida in 2011, a police officer was cleaning his firearm in a school when it discharged. While no one was injured, the incident had the potential for a more deadly outcome. In some

Birmingham, Alabama schools, police have used pepper spray against students, leading to multiple injuries.

Tasers, however, have remained at the forefront of the controversy around the use of police weapons within schools. For many police officers, the Taser is "just another tool in the hands of law enforcement that we have in our options other than the use of deadly force."[2] For some parents and guardians, however, the Taser is a weapon that may one day be used against their child. The continuing controversy speaks to the ongoing effort to clarify the use of Tasers in schools and elsewhere.

Notes

1. Jack Leonard and Richard Winston, "Hawthorne Police Review Use of Taser on Middle School Student," *Los Angeles Times*, March 2, 2009. (http://articles.latimes.com/2009/mar/02/local/me-taser2)

2. Annie Martin, "Tasers Coming to Flager Schools," *News Journal Online*, October 6, 2011. (http://www.news journalonline.com/news/local/flagler/2011/10/06/tasers -coming-to-flagler-schools.html)

1

Tasers and Stun Guns: An Overview

Canadian Broadcasting Corporation (CBC) News

The Canadian Broadcasting Corporation (CBC) is a public broadcasting company in Canada first established in 1936.

A Taser is a stun gun made by Taser International, an Arizona-based company. Tasers have become very popular with law enforcement in the United States and other countries. A Taser typically ejects two probes that deliver an electrical jolt, temporarily incapacitating the person shot. The Taser has both benefits and drawbacks. While Tasers have worked as safer substitutes for firearms in many incidents, critics note that there has been little testing to assure that Tasers are safe. It is also uncertain whether Tasers deliver a higher voltage than advertised by the manufacturer. Taser use has also been a factor in a number of injuries and deaths.

Tasers are hand-held weapons that deliver a jolt of electricity through a pair of wires propelled by compressed air from up to 10.6 metres away.

The jolt stuns the target by causing an uncontrollable contraction of the muscle tissue. The target is immobilized and falls to the ground—regardless of pain tolerance or mental focus.

Taser stands for "Thomas A. Swift Electric Rifle." It is named after a series of children's science-fiction novels written in the early 20th century featuring the young genius inventor Tom Swift.

Who Makes Tasers?

Arizona-based Taser International makes virtually all of the stun guns being used today. The technical term for a stun gun is a "conducted energy device" (CED) or "conducted energy weapon" (CEW).

Taser International says more than 16,200 law enforcement agencies in more than 40 countries use its devices. Since early 1998, more than 543,000 Taser brand immobilizers have been sold to law enforcement agencies.

There are five main types of stun guns made by Taser used by law enforcement agencies:

- M26: A high-powered weapon marketed to police forces to stop "highly combative individuals." A burst of compressed nitrogen launches two small probes attached to the device by conductive wires. From as far as 10.6 metres, the device transmits electrical pulses through the wires to immobilize a person. Also has a laser sight for aiming.

Since early 1998, more than 543,000 Taser brand immobilizers have been sold to law enforcement agencies.

- X26: A smaller model introduced in 2003. Launches two small probes as far as 10.6 metres.

- X3: A triple-shot semi-automatic introduced in 2009. Capable of deploying three separate sets of two small probes as far as 10.6 metres as a backup shot in the event of a miss or to stop up to three separate targets.

- X2: A double-shot semi-automatic introduced in 2011. Capable of deploying two separate sets of two small probes as far as 10.6 metres as a backup shot in the event of a miss or to stop up to two separate targets.

- XREP: A CED projectile deployed by a pump action 12-guage shotgun round capable of hitting targets as far away as 30 metres.

The company also makes stun guns for personal use:

- C2: Introduced in 2007, smaller than its predecessors and comes in nine colours. Launches two probes as far as 4.5 metres.

- X26C: Modelled after the X26 but formatted for personal use. Has a range of 4.5 metres.

- Advanced Taser M18/M18L: Modelled after the M26 with a range of 4.5 metres.

In the United States, Tasers are not considered firearms and are legal for civilian use in most states. Some cities, counties and states do restrict—or ban—their use by people who are not police officers. The company will not ship its product outside the United States unless the person placing the order holds a valid import/export permit.

In Canada, however, Tasers are a prohibited weapon. Only one company can import them into Canada under a special permit, and they can only sell the devices to law enforcement agencies, said RCMP [Royal Canadian Mounted Police] Cpl. Greg Gillis, who trains police officers in how to use Tasers. Each Taser sale is registered and tracked, much like a handgun, he said.

In 2010, 79 per cent of the company's $86.9 million US in revenue came from sales within the United States.

What Are the Benefits of Stun Guns?

Tasers are supposed to allow police officers to subdue violent individuals without killing them. A police officer can "take down" a threatening suspect without worrying that a stray bullet might kill or injure an innocent bystander.

"There's no question that there are certainly lots of documented examples in Canada where had we not had the Taser and had to respond with more traditional options, that it could have resulted in a higher level of force," said Gillis. "For example, the firearm: . . . with a firearm, there are only two outcomes . . . it's going to be a permanent injury or a loss of life."

"We don't speak often enough about the number of lives that have been saved, the number of people that are up and walking around today that might not have been had it not been for a Taser," says Steve Palmer, executive director of the Canadian Police Research Centre [CPRC]. The CPRC is a partnership among the Canadian Association of Chiefs of Police, the RCMP and the National Research Council of Canada.

What Are the Drawbacks of Stun Guns?

The company says there are none and that Taser devices are among the safest use-of-force options available. Critics argue that there hasn't been enough research into the safety of stun guns.

Amnesty International says that between 2001 and August 2008, 334 Americans died after Taser shocks. The stun gun was deemed to have caused or contributed to at least 50 of those deaths, Amnesty says, citing medical examiners and coroners. Most suspects were unarmed, and many were subjected to repeated or prolonged shocks, according to Amnesty.

Critics argue that there hasn't been enough research into the safety of stun guns.

The human rights group has called for governments to limit the use of stun guns or suspend their use.

In November 2007, the UN [United Nations] Committee Against Torture released a statement saying "use of Taser X26 weapons, provoking extreme pain, constituted a form of torture, and . . . in certain cases, it could also cause death."

In June 2008, Taser International lost its first civil suit. The company was ordered to pay more than $5 million in damages after a jury in San Jose, Calif., found that shocks from the company's devices contributed 15 per cent to the Feb. 19, 2005, death of Robert Heston, 40. The jury found that Heston's own actions, including toxic methamphetamine ingestion, were 85 per cent responsible for his death.

The jury determined the company was negligent for failing to warn police that prolonged deployment of the stun gun could increase the risk of cardiac arrest.

The exact cause of death has often been contentious in cases involving Tasers.

In July 2005, for example, a Chicago medical examiner ruled that the death of a man in February 2005 was the result of being shot with a Taser by Chicago police. Media reports said it was the first time a death had been linked directly to a police stun gun, although the medical examiner said the victim also had a lot of methamphetamine in his system.

On Oct. 14, 2007, Robert Dziekanski, 40, of Pieszyce, Poland, died at Vancouver International Airport after being shocked five times with a Taser by RCMP officers.

Excited delirium is described as an agitated state in which a person experiences an irregular heartbeat and suddenly dies.

Airport security called the RCMP for help after Dziekanski allegedly was pounding on windows and throwing chairs and computer equipment.

Initially, the Mounties speculated that he died from a rare condition called excited delirium. Excited delirium is described as an agitated state in which a person experiences an irregular heartbeat and suddenly dies. It can happen to psychiatric patients and people using drugs such as cocaine. But critics charge that excited delirium is not a valid medical term.

A coroner concluded Dziekanski died as a result of the stress from both the Taser stuns and the struggle as they pinned him to the ground and handcuffed him.

How Much Electricity Does a Taser Use?

News reports will often quote the voltage delivered by a Taser—up to 50,000 volts. That sounds like a lot of electricity, but it's a misleading way of expressing the power a Taser uses.

Tasers work by passing electricity through a pair of wires. Weighted barbed hooks at the ends of the wires are propelled toward the target by compressed air.

Tasers are designed to incapacitate a person through up to five centimetres of clothing. Taser International says the electrical pulse is delivered at a high voltage because the electric current has to pass through clothing and air—neither of which is a good conductor of electricity—to make a complete circuit with the target's skin.

Taser International also says that while its device can deliver up to 50,000 volts in an open air arc only, it does not deliver that much voltage to a person's body. The company says its Taser X26 delivers an average of 1,200 volts.

As well, the high-voltage pulse of a Taser is said to carry only a small current, typically 0.002 to 0.03 amps.

By comparison, electrical outlets in Canada deliver 120 volts of electricity, and the current they carry depends on the appliance that's plugged into them. A 60-watt light bulb, for example, pulls 0.5 amps, while a toaster pulls about five amps.

It's possible to suffer a fatal shock from a household electrical socket, at just 120 volts with 15 amps, if enough current passes through the body.

Tests conducted for CBC News/Radio-Canada, however, found that some stun guns produced higher-than-advertised current.

The procedures, conducted by U.S.-based lab National Technical Systems, found that 10 per cent of the X26 model Tasers produced more electrical current than the weapon's specifications.

In some cases, the current was up to 50 per cent stronger than specified. The X26 Tasers were manufactured before 2005 and are one of the most commonly used models.

Taser International said CBC made scientific errors by failing to spark-test the weapons before firing them, a process the company recommends police officers do on a regular basis. But engineers who reviewed the testing protocol for CBC said the tests were based on solid practices.

2

Tasers Are Safe When Used Properly

Jeffrey D. Ho

Jeffrey D. Ho is an emergency physician at Hennepin County Medical Center in Minneapolis.

While Tasers are basically safe, it is necessary for Taser International to periodically provide information on best practices. Updating best practices does not mean that Tasers were unsafe in the past. Rather, as more testing has been completed, the company better understands how to most effectively use the weapons it manufactures. Likewise, it is misleading to assume that any weapon should meet a "zero risk" standard. Tasers are frequently used in situations involving violence and aggression, and while the use of stun guns occasionally leads to injury, Tasers also have the potential to save lives. Many of the recommendations of Taser International are designed to make the Taser more effective for law enforcement, and should not be viewed as an admission that the weapon is in any way unsafe.

I am an emergency medicine physician and a law enforcement officer. These two professions leave no doubt that my roles on this planet are to serve and observe.

While serving others, I have had the privilege of observing many things about people in crisis and society in general and if I had to distill my observations down to two main points, they would be:

Jeffrey D. Ho, "Best Practices in Taser Targeting," *Police Magazine*, January 30, 2010. www.policemag.com. Copyright © 2010 by *Police Magazine*. All rights reserved. Reproduced by permission.

- People often need to be saved from themselves.

- Miscommunication and misunderstanding is at the root of every crisis.

I cannot change human behavior so point one is really more like a permanent law of society, and I view it as favorable to my job security. However, point two can and should be corrected when it occurs.

The ability for these devices to gain compliance when used properly while reducing officer and suspect injuries is remarkable.

Over the past five years, I have had the privilege of working very closely with all of the technology that TASER International has brought to the field of law enforcement. I have used some of it in training and some of it while on the job. I have played with all of it in the research lab, and I have been called upon on many occasions to talk and teach about what I know and what I have learned regarding this technology. It has been interesting to see how the evolution of this technology has changed the way that law enforcement does its job. The ability for these devices to gain compliance when used properly while reducing officer and suspect injuries is remarkable.

As part of the evolution of TASER technology and tactics, a recent training bulletin was issued by TASER International to update users about what is believed to be the current best practice. This bulletin has been interpreted differently by agencies and individuals. Some of the misinterpretations span the spectrum from "No changes, business as usual" to "We are totally banning these devices from use at our agency." As in almost every situation that has this much polarity, the truth lies somewhere in the middle.

I have had many cops, chiefs, docs, nurses, attorneys, and reporters contact me to ask for my opinions of TASER's new training advisory. The one thing that is clear from their questions and comments is that the bulletin has many statements and details that educated people did not fully understand and that the media reported incorrectly.

As I stated above, a crisis that stems from miscommunication or misunderstanding deserves to be corrected when it occurs. This led me to make a list of items from this training bulletin that need more detailed explanation. They are as follows:

The TASER Training Bulletin is intended as a "best practices" update for the end user.

It was not intended as an admission of a conspiracy or some type of manufacturer disclosure. I should know since I helped to write it.

The bulletin was based on evolving knowledge of the research available and from field experiences with the TASER devices. I tell people to look at it as if the manufacturer is continually updating information for the end user as a recommendation for best practice.

My colleagues in medicine will understand this because health care professionals are subject to these types of practice updates on a regular basis.

For instance, over the years the practice of CPR [cardiopulmonary resuscitation] has changed and will continue to do so. Every so often the American Heart Association reviews all of the data known about CPR and makes new recommendations about CPR such as the recommended rate of compressions, compression-to-breathing ratio, proper ventilation, etc. CPR in the year 2010 is not the same CPR that was taught in 1980. These changes reflect the best practice of this life-saving maneuver. They do not mean that the CPR performed 10 years ago was harmful. They mean that we now know more information about CPR and have more experience with it to make better recommendations.

Another good analogy to this is automobile airbags. When airbags were initially introduced in the 1980s, they were installed for the front seat only and came with no recommendations, restrictions, or other instructions for the end user. The motorist simply drove and when an appropriate collision happened, the bag deployed.

[I]n the future, there will continue to be other evolving recommendations for TASER devices . . . .

As experience and crash data became available, we began to see refinements and best practice recommendations from the auto industry in this area such as advisements about not sitting too close to the dashboard or steering wheel, not storing items that can become projectiles on the dashboards, keeping your hands on the ring of the steering wheel instead of the center where the bag deploys, etc. All of these recommendations came in the form of evolving updates from the auto industry for best practice standards.

These two analogies from other fields show that best practices evolve, which is the reason why TASER sent out its recent training bulletin. I expect that in the future, there will continue to be other evolving recommendations for TASER devices too.

People seem to be fixated to a fanatical degree about TASER devices and risk.

For some reason, many people (including supposed educated experts) expect that the use of a TASER device should equate to a "zero risk" process.

To keep this in perspective, it is important to remember that TASER devices are designed for deployment in very high-risk situations involving acts of violence and aggression. The very nature of the typical scenario means that the situation is already fairly high risk to both the suspect and the law enforcement personnel involved.

A TASER device is a tool of force that is used tactically to gain control of persons that require force to comply with the lawful orders of a police office. People need to understand that there will never be "zero risk" when a TASER device is used.

However, if you look at all of the animal and human study data on this subject and the surveillance data from real field use over the past several years, the risk of an adverse event is really very low when compared with the alternative options. These options include allowing for continued agitation and resistance by the suspect, which would result in profound metabolic acidosis; use of blunt force such as a fist or impact baton that would result in a high likelihood of trauma; use of a firearm that involves a very high probability of death or permanent disability.

> *People need to understand that there will never be "zero risk" when a TASER device is used.*

When you look at the risk-benefit ratio of TASER device use, it becomes much easier to understand that the risk is acceptable because it is low and the benefit to all involved is high in terms of injury prevention.

The reason that the "Preferred Targeting" zones are now in the training bulletin is primarily for risk management.

In reviewing litigation involving TASER International as well as litigation involving only law enforcement agencies, it seems that the area of the chest is a point of fixation for litigation. If there is a death involved, the argument is that the area of the chest is dangerous and the person's heart was electrocuted. In cases of TASER device use where there is no death, the argument is that because the chest was targeted, there was intent on the officer's part to potentially use this as a lethal form of force from attempted electrocution and therefore the officer used excessive force.

The research data does not support the chest as being a consistently dangerous area to apply a TASER device. There have been cases of abnormal heartbeats from a TASER device applied to small swine, and I would not say that the risk of this is zero in a human.

However, I would say that the human research and field surveillance data of chest applications does not support that this is consistently happening so the risk would be extremely small. In fact, respected researchers in this area state that the possibility of a TASER device application to the chest causing a fatal heart rhythm is in the range of 0.0000014 to 0.000011. This is such a small number that it essentially rounds to zero.

Still despite this extremely minute number, moving the preferred area of aim lower than the chest when possible is a good idea. Doing so neutralizes the entire argument of chest application being dangerous and TASER believes this will go a long way in preventing unnecessary litigation that plagues its law enforcement customers.

Moving the point of aim lower when practical is also an evolutionary best practice from an injury standpoint.

There have been a number of cases where an officer was aiming a TASER at a suspect's center chest and when the device was fired, the dart ended up striking the subject in an area that would be considered undesirable such as the eye, the skull, the throat, and neck.

When the officer targets a subject's chest with the TASER's laser aiming device, the subject often decides to move aggressively toward the officer. Such aggressive moves are typically done by lowering the head to charge at the officer. The officer then reacts to this aggressive action and deploys the TASER device at the subject's center mass. But because the head has been lowered, the top dart strikes the subject in the head, face, or neck.

Lowering the preferred point of aim by a few inches will minimize these types of undesirable shots. Again, this is a best practice recommendation based on field experience. By adhering to this when possible, you are less likely to incur a dart embedment into a sensitive area and this lessens the liability risk for you and your agency.

Lowering the point of aim improves the incapacitation effect of the TASER device application.

One of the most effective applications is to have the TASER darts embed in areas of large skeletal muscle mass.

Based on experience both in the research lab and in real field encounters, this is another example of how the best practice recommendation is evolving.

One of the most effective applications is to have the TASER darts embed in areas of large skeletal muscle mass. For instance, since TASER International's devices have been in production, the human back has always been taught to be a preferred target area because of all the skeletal muscles located on either side that run the entire length of the spine. These muscles are used for balance and erect posture. When you can affect these with the TASER device, the person loses the ability to stand up and you get the desired effect of causing them to fall down and lose control of themselves. When you don't affect these areas, the person has a higher chance of still being able to continue with his or her undesirable behavior or to remove the darts. Because of this, the back of the subject remains a preferred area for application. There is nothing new about this recommendation.

We have also discovered that for a frontal shot, one of the highest percentages of successful neuromuscular incapacitation occurs when you "split the beltline." That means you put one dart above the belt into the muscles of the abdomen and one dart below the belt into the muscles of the pelvic girdle or the thighs. The muscles in these areas are also used for erect posture and balance.

Splitting the belt line is much more effective than firing the TASER into the subject's chest. In general, the muscles located in the chest are not very large. This means the TASER effect is less likely to incapacitate the subject. There are many reported cases of persons removing the darts from the chest area on their own and continuing their undesirable behaviors. Lowering the preferred target area increases the chance of successful belt splitting by the user.

The training bulletin gives best practice recommendations, not absolutes and does not prohibit shots to the chest.

In other words, the bulletin recommends that the chest is not a preferred target area for all of the reasons discussed above. It does not, however, prohibit chest shots. In fact, it actually recognizes that in many situations, an officer will not be able to avoid a chest shot because of movement, dynamics of the scenario, tactical issues, and/or time. In those situations, there is nothing that states that an application to the chest is off-limits.

As this bulletin was being written, it was recognized that using prohibitive language would only serve to box in officers and make them apprehensive about using their TASER devices. It is unfortunate, however, that many agencies have misunderstood this point and decided to make large, sweeping changes because of this misunderstanding such as removing TASER devices from their officers or writing their policies to be more restrictive. Officer and suspect injury rates will escalate when those types of reactionary and reflexive decisions are made without fully understanding the issue.

What the bulletin does recommend, however, is that when officers have the luxury of time and can aim to place a shot, they should try to follow the preferred targeting recommendations for optimal results and risk management. This is really no different than saying when you have the time and can line up your shot, you may want to try to target the back with the TASER device because that also has a very high likelihood of best effect. The bulletin is all about improving the user's odds of success while minimizing risk and liability based on evolving information.

The training bulletin is also promoting a universal target scheme for ease of operator use.

TASER International now has several products available for law enforcement use. One of them is the shotgun propelled XREP device, which has the characteristics of blunt impact as well as electrical charge delivery for incapacitation.

When you look at all of the propelled impact tools available (bean bag rounds, ferret rounds, baton rounds, sock rounds, etc.), all of them recommend that you avoid shooting a blunt impact device at the head or chest and that the desired point of aim is slightly lower than that. This is true for the XREP device also and it is not optimal for TASER International to teach officers to aim at different areas of a person depending on which product is in use.

To avoid confusion, it is felt that having a preferred universal targeting scheme for all of its devices would be easiest for the officers to train with, remember, and use. Therefore, it was decided that the training bulletin should give this universal preferred targeting scheme from here on out for all of its devices.

Hopefully, this has helped give you a better understanding of the recent TASER International training bulletin and will allow you and your agencies to make more informed decisions about usage and policy.

3

Tasers Are Unsafe Even When Used Properly

James Hibberd

James Hibberd is a senior reporter for Television Week *magazine, and has written for the* New York Times, Salon, *and* Details.

While Taser International has asserted that its weapons are safe, many critics note that the company's stun gun has injured and killed a number of persons. At the beginning of 2009, over 90 people had died in the United States and Canada after being stunned, and the Taser has been frequently used against unarmed citizens. Taser International worked hard to convince law enforcement to use its stun guns for a number of years before finding success during the late 1990s. While Tasers became popular with the police and the military, however, there was little testing data to support the company's safety claims. Because of the lack of accurate testing data, Amnesty International has called for a moratorium on Tasers. Until testing can be completed, Tasers should be considered unsafe and not marketed to either law enforcement or the public.

Sgt. Samuel Powers loved being a cop. A 15-year veteran of the Maricopa County, Ariz., Sheriff's Department, Powers likes to say that he never spent a day at work. "I loved this job more than anything else in the world," he said.

Three years ago, Powers' department was issued the M26 Tasers—gun-like stun weapons that fire 50,000 volts of electricity via two wires led by piercing darts.

James Hibberd, "Aftershocks," *Amnesty International*, January 6, 2009. www.amnesty usa.org.

"I heard they were the best thing to ever happen to law enforcement," Powers said. "I was told it was a new weapon that was nonlethal, that it absolutely could not hurt anybody."

During his mandatory training class, Powers watched as one officer after another experienced the Taser's shock. Full-grown men, tough cops, were taken down in a flash with an embarrassing involuntary holler as an electric charge scrambles their nervous system.

When it was Powers' turn, the weapon's electrodes were attached to his ankle and shoulder. His captain pulled the trigger.

And what happened next changed Powers forever.

"Instantly I was in severe pain," he said. "The next thing I knew, I was on the ground. Just trying to draw breath killed me. The pain radiated around from my back and chest. It was the worst pain I ever felt in my life." A doctor told Powers the muscle contractions caused by the Taser's electrical charge had crushed one of his thoracic vertebrae. His career as a cop was over.

And yet—Powers was one of the lucky ones.

Taser-Related Deaths

More than 90 people have died in the United States and Canada after being struck with a Taser, which is manufactured, marketed and sold by the Arizona-based Taser International.

Nobody is entirely sure whether the Taser caused their deaths, or if a confluence of unique medical factors was the culprit. For all their dramatic power, there is a surprising lack of scientific research documenting the physiological impact of the Taser charge. Yet for years the weapon has been promoted to law enforcement and civilians as a safe alternative to lethal force.

Amnesty International (AI) has tracked Tasers for years. As the popularity of Tasers skyrocketed among U.S. law enforcement agencies during the past few years, deaths associated with the weapons have likewise increased—along with clear examples of abuse. Amnesty's latest report, released in November [2009], documented police officers using Tasers against an intoxicated man strapped to a hospital gurney; a 50-year-old man who refused to give police his date of birth at a picnic; and a woman six months pregnant, shocked in the abdomen, while handcuffed and seated in the back of a police car.

[T]here is a surprising lack of scientific research documenting the physiological impact of the Taser change.

In 80 percent of cases, the Amnesty report said, suspects were unarmed. In 36 percent of cases, the weapons were used due to "verbal noncompliance." Mark Silverstein, legal director of the ACLU [American Civil Liberties Union] in Colorado, cited Amnesty International's report in a campaign to urge Denver police to increase their threat threshold for using Tasers.

"Tasers are promoted as a less lethal alternative to firearms in cases where police would otherwise use deadly force," Silverstein said. "But what many people are unaware of is Tasers are used in numerous situations where even your most rogue cowboy-type officer wouldn't even dream of pulling a firearm. And even if it doesn't cause death, it's still 50,000 volts of electricity that cause immediate, overwhelming and excruciating pain that is disproportionate to the need for it."

The efforts of AI and other campaigner have not gone unnoticed. In [2008-2009], several media outlets have published in-depth investigative reports documenting Taser abuse and deaths. Taser International shareholders have filed more than one dozen class-action lawsuits against the company, accusing Taser of making misleading claims about the safety of its guns in order to maintain profitability.

And even some law enforcement agencies—Taser's most voracious customers and vigorous defenders—are now having second thoughts about a weapon that has become standard issue equipment for about 100,000 police officers across the country.

The Taser Success Story

Benjamin Franklin discovered the electrical nature of lightning in 1752. But people were shocking each other with electricity as far back as 3000 B.C. The effect of electricity is dramatic because the human body is an electrical system suspended in salt water. Introducing an outside charge—especially a 50,000 volt shock from a device like the Taser—instantly overwhelms your system, and your mind loses control of your body.

In 1974 a Hughes Aerospace physicist named Jack Cover recognized that electricity, properly administered, could act as an effective weapon. He invented an electroshock device and named it after a series of Tom Swift adventure books he read as a kid. Taser is an acronym for "Tom Swift's Electric Rifle."

Law enforcement agencies liked the concept but were unimpressed by the execution of the early stun gun. Sales were sluggish. In 1993, two brothers, Patrick and Tom Smith, bought the Taser technology. Working out of Cover's garage, the Smiths formed Air Taser. For several years they struggled to gain the respect of law enforcement without success.

Then, in 1999, the company developed its most powerful stun weapon yet—the Advanced M26 Taser. The new Tasers looked and felt like real guns and boasted 94 percent effectiveness in stopping a suspect. Police liked the look, the feel and the results.

In 2001 Rick Smith declared in a newspaper interview: "This is the gun of the future." And he was right. Sales rocketed from $2.2 million in 1999 to $24.5 million in 2003 to $67.7 million last year [2008]. Air Taser changed its name to

Taser International and began exporting its weapons to law enforcement agencies worldwide.

In thousands of U.S. markets, residents saw variations of the same story in their newspaper. The police department has new non-lethal weapons. Officers are excited to have another effective tool to stop crime. Anecdotes and statistics demonstrate how Tasers have saved the lives of reckless police suspects without injury.

However, in many markets, the story of "Police Issued Stun Guns" was followed by another story. The names change, but the headline is remarkably consistent: "Man Dies After Police Use Stun Gun."

Taser's primary research . . . consisted of a company-paid farmer and doctor shocking a single pig in 1996 and five dogs in 1999 to see if the weapon would cause cardiac arrest.

Inaccurate Testing Data

When Taser International introduced the M26, the company assured customers the weapon had passed several safety tests and the shocks were not strong enough to cause any permanent damage.

Taser's primary research however, consisted of a company-paid farmer and doctor shocking a single pig in 1996 and five dogs in 1999 to see if the weapon would cause cardiac arrest. The tests were not published for independent review.

Additional studies did not prove Tasers safe, either. A 1989 Canadian study found Tasers caused heart attacks in pigs with pacemakers. A 1999 Department of Justice study found an electronic device weaker than the Taser can cause cardiac arrest in people with heart conditions. A 2002 study by the British government concluded, "The high-power Tasers cannot be classed, in the vernacular, as 'safe.'"

The most recent major study was conducted by a division of the Department of Defense last year [2008], but it was not publicly released. Taser declared the report determined Tasers "will generally be effective . . . without a significant risk of unintended severe effects."

But the Air Force scientist who conducted the study has said otherwise. According to media reports, the study actually found Tasers caused heart damage in pigs, that more research on the weapons was needed and that Taser victims should receive medical monitoring.

It wasn't the first time a medical professional has been caught in the middle of the Taser controversy. Last year [in 2008] a South Carolina coroner said that Taser pressured his office to reverse an autopsy report that stated the Taser's electrical charge contributed to a man's death. Researchers for Underwriters Laboratories discovered Taser was using their research on electrical fences to claim stun guns were safe enough to shock a two year old.

"They used our information, saying what's good for electric fences is good for Taser," said Underwriters Laboratories spokesperson Paul Baker. "We felt it was very misleading; it's apples and oranges." To some, the fact there is any debate as to the weapon's effectiveness is itself cause for concern.

Researchers for Underwriters Laboratories discovered Taser was using their research on electrical fences to claim stun guns were safe enough to shock a two year old.

Tom Aveni, 23-year police trainer with the Police Policy Studies Council in New Mexico, calls the Taser research "disjointed and compartmentalized."

"The major source of information on Taser is Taser International itself," Aveni said. "Every major study has either been directly or indirectly funded or influenced by Taser. There just hasn't been enough independent research to set the record straight."

Calling for a Moratorium on Tasers

Until there is, Amnesty International has called for a moratorium on the use of stun weapons until a rigorous, independent study of their use and effects can be completed. Failing that, AI recommends law enforcement agencies establish policies limiting use to situations in which the weapons are an alternative to deadly force, and create mechanisms for oversight and accountability when officers violate these policies.

Though Taser International did not return calls for this story, CEO Rick Smith has released statements about AI's stance. "Amnesty International should support a life saving technology used by law enforcement to reduce suspect and officer injuries and one that has saved thousands of suspect lives," Smith said.

William F. Schulz, executive director of Amnesty International USA, counters: "Our only issue is that Tasers are distributed, marketed and utilized at such a rapidly growing rate, and there remains so much uncertainty in regard to their full health implications. After all, the world went for how many hundreds of years without police officers having Tasers at their disposal."

More Testing Is Needed

Since 1999 the number of people who died after being shot by Tasers has climbed steadily. But they usually don't die for a few minutes or an hour after the charge. Also, people who die after receiving a Taser shock typically have underlying medical problems or were on stimulating drugs such as cocaine or PCP at the time.

For years Taser officials insisted that no medical examination of a shock victim had ever cited their guns for causing "injury or death to another human being." But a 2004 investigation by *The Arizona Republic* found Taser never saw the autopsy reports, instead relying on media accounts and police anecdotes. After an exhaustive search, *The Republic* linked the guns to 94 deaths in the United States and Canada since 1999—similar to AI's findings.

Most medical examiners cited the primary cause of death as cardiac arrest, drug intoxication or positional asphyxiation. In at least 12 deaths, medical examiners listed the Taser as a contributing factor. One theory is that a pre-existing condition or drug use, combined with shock from a Taser during a period of anxiety or exertion—such as resisting arrest—can bring about increased acidosis in the blood, leading to death. Such conditions have also resulted in the sudden death of police suspects and prisoners without the use of a stun gun. "I think what we're seeing with Taser is an exacerbation of pre-existing conditions," Aveni said.

Since 1999 the number of people who died after being shot by Tasers has climbed steadily.

But which pre-existing conditions put people at risk? What is the weapon's effect on people with a heart condition? With osteoporosis? How do you medically treat a person after he has received a shock?

There are significant research studies underway to explore such issues. The questions have prompted the largest association of police chiefs to issue a national bulletin in February urging police departments to review their use of stun guns while the association studies Taser related deaths.

Bill Lewinski, executive director of the Force Science Research Center at Minnesota State University, believes Taser has been "oversold as a safe instrument" and has called for more research. Yet Lewinski draws a hard line against taking the weapons away from police officers, an idea he said "would literally create a catastrophe for peace officers."

"Taser was remiss in not doing more research," Lewinski said. "But Amnesty International is remiss in calling for a moratorium on a useful tool that's saved a lot of lives."

There's at least one cop—one former cop—who disagrees, however.

"Did my opinion [of the Taser] change?" mused Powers, the officer whose vertebrae was crushed during his training test.

"Well, you know, it did," he said. "I believed what they told me. They told me it couldn't hurt me. As time went on, I did more research, and I realized Taser was not tested on people. This thing should have been completely and fully tested by somebody before it went out on the market. I assumed it had already been done. Nobody knows completely what this thing does. Nobody. And that puts the public and law enforcement at risk. Take this thing off the market until it's been tested."

4

Excited Delirium Is an Ill-Defined Phenomenon Used to Explain Taser Deaths

Bernice Yeung

Bernice Yeung is a journalist focusing on social issues and has written a number of articles for Mother Jones.

While Taser International has stated that its stun guns are safe, a number of people have died after being stunned. The company has blamed these deaths on excited delirium (ED), a phenomenon that has also been associated with cocaine deaths. However, ED is difficult to define and the problem becomes more complicated because the symptoms are so varied that they are almost meaningless. While ED has a long history, a number of observers believe that Taser International has popularized the syndrome. The company has also been helped in this cause by a number of experts who publically advance the syndrome. The experts, however, also have close ties to Taser International which creates a conflict of interest. Despite these conflicts, Taser has been mostly successful in moving the spotlight away from itself and placing it on ED.

By all accounts, Patrick Lee was having too good a time at the Mercy Lounge, a Nashville rock club. He'd commenced the September 2005 evening by dropping a few hits of acid. Before long, the 21-year-old was tripping and determined to climb onstage. A bouncer eighty-sixed him and called the cops, who, according to witnesses, found Lee outside the club, babbling incoherently. Things went downhill fast. Lee made a move toward an officer and was hit with pepper spray. He ran a few feet and stripped off his clothes. The cops deployed their Tasers, jolting Lee 19 times in all. By the time paramedics arrived, witnesses say, he was unresponsive. He died 39 hours later. The cause, a county medical examiner concluded, was "excited delirium."

For the past five years, this has been a common conclusion in deadly incidents involving Tasers, and the nation's top seller of electric stun guns prefers it that way; Taser International Inc. has twice sued medical examiners who cited its products as a contributing factor in a subject's death. At the same time, the company aggressively promotes awareness of excited delirium, an ill-defined condition that helps it fend off lawsuits. Thanks partly to testimony from a cast of ED proponents, several with financial ties to the company, Taser has lost just one wrongful-death case at trial out of 33 filed against it since 2001. (Dozens more lawsuits are pending.)

Amnesty International . . . says there have been 334 fatalities following Taser jolts since 2001.

Taser's lone courtroom defeat, which it may appeal, involves Robert Heston, a California meth user who died after 25 jolts. Last June [2008], the family's lawyers convinced a jury that Heston most likely died not of ED, but rather of cardiac arrest due to metabolic acidosis—a temporary state in agitated individuals that may be exacerbated by excessive Tasering, recent animal studies indicate. But in January [2009], a suit by Patrick Lee's parents was dismissed after Taser argued that excited delirium was the culprit. "We look at excited delirium as a responsibility-shifting mechanism," says Peter Williamson, an attorney for the Hestons. "It's a way for the police department, the officer, and Taser to shift responsibility to the victim."

The company insists its devices never kill, but Amnesty International, the only organization to have compiled data on the issue, says there have been 334 fatalities following Taser jolts since 2001. In 69 of these cases, autopsy reports specifically cited ED as a cause of death.

Defining Excited Delirium

"Of all in-custody deaths [not involving firearms], excited delirium syndrome is the most common form," notes Vincent Di Maio, a Taser expert witness, retired Texas medical examiner, and coauthor of the 2005 book *Excited Delirium Syndrome: Cause of Death and Prevention.*

But as a medical condition, the term is meaningless. "We have no idea what any of the causes are, what the biology behind it might be, what underlies it, how being in this state leads to death with supposedly some intervention with a Taser or other force," says Matthew Stanbrook, a faculty member at the University of Toronto medical school.

Purported ED signs range from "bizarre" behavior to sweating and high body temperature, attraction to shiny objects or glass, foaming at the mouth, a penchant for disrobing, aggression, and superhuman strength. Such symptoms could result from "alcohol withdrawal, acute schizophrenia, bipolar disease, stimulant drug intoxication, psychological illness plus stimulant drugs, hypoglycemia, an infection of the brain. I could go on," says Christine Hall, a Canadian ER physician who researches in-custody deaths.

"The bottom line is this," says Andrew Dennis, a Chicago surgeon, part-time police officer, and medical researcher who coauthored three studies of Taser's effects on swine. "You have a lot of people who are acting psychotic, and often law enforcement is asked to deal with them. Some subgroup of this population is going to die, and we don't know why. This potential at-risk group is the quote-unquote excited delirium group. But there are no common threads to identify this at-risk group. As far as I'm concerned, everything discussed about excited delirium is conjecture."

None of these concerns have stopped Taser from talking up ED in training sessions, literature, and court filings. The company attends conferences for police chiefs and medical examiners, where it distributes ED-related literature, and has doled out free copies of Di Maio's book. It also sends unsolicited materials to medical examiners when an in-custody death occurs in their jurisdiction. In 2002, Taser released a statement for police to use if someone died in a Taser-related incident. "We regret the unfortunate loss of life," it begins. "There are many cases where excited delirium caused by various mental disorders or medical conditions, that may or may not include drug use, can lead to a fatal conclusion."

Several people . . . credit Taser for helping popularize excited delirium.

The History of Excited Delirium

The expression first appeared in medical documents in the 1800s, and for a time it was associated with deaths in asylums. It fell into disuse during the 1950s and was revived in the 1980s, essentially to describe the agitated state of cocaine addicts. Since then, ED has been the subject of dozens of articles aimed at law enforcement. (Among the authors are Jeffrey Ho, an ER doctor whom Taser pays to conduct studies and testify—he got $70,000 during a recent 12-month stretch—and Mark Kroll, a member of Taser's science advisory board who has cashed in at least $2.5 million in company stock options.)

The term has also gained traction among medical examiners and coroners. "People are looking for an explanation for some of these deaths," notes Stanbrook, "and this syndrome provides an answer that's convenient." (In an unpublished survey last year [in 2008] by a national medical examiners group,

67 of 187 MEs [medical examiner] said Taser's litigiousness would affect their conclusions in cases involving stun guns.) Last October [2008], prompted by the term's growing popularity in law enforcement, the American College of Emergency Physicians resolved to study whether ED should be considered as a diagnosis.

Several people I spoke with credit Taser for helping popularize excited delirium. Dennis, the surgeon-cop, first heard the term, he says, at a company training session five years ago; Shao-Hua Lu, a psychiatrist who treats addicts at Vancouver General Hospital, hadn't heard of ED before 2007, when he began working on a Canadian government probe of Taser safety. "No [practicing] medical doctor would write down 'delirium' on a death certificate as a cause of death," says Lu, who trains Canadian Mounties to identify mental health problems, including various forms of delirium, in their subjects. "I don't understand why MEs would write that."

Promoting Excited Delirium

Taser insists that any corporate outreach involving ED relates to safe use of its products. "We don't teach anything about excited delirium," says spokesman Steve Turtle. "We let law enforcement agencies know that they need to be aware of it."

But the company is remarkably tight with America's foremost ED training and advocacy business. The Institute for the Prevention of In-Custody Deaths (ipicd) was cofounded by police trainer John Peters and an old acquaintance, Michael Brave, Taser's national litigation counsel.

At the time, Peters later stated in a deposition, he was reworking his firm's training regimen after hearing from other stun-gun merchants. "Some of the manufacturers said, you know, '[Police departments] are paying out lots of money in these lawsuits, and it's hurting us because they don't have money left over to buy our product.'"

In 2005, Peters filed corporate papers for the ipicd listing himself and Brave as the founding directors. Within six months, the institute was leading eight-hour sessions at Taser's Scottsdale, Arizona, compound, teaching cops to recognize ED and often touting Tasers as the most effective tool for subduing agitated individuals. In the first two years, Brave estimated in a deposition, Taser paid $70,000 to $80,000 for the sessions. To date, Peters says, the ipicd has certified some 10,000 officers worldwide as in-custody death prevention instructors.

Taser also pays the way for Peters and ipicd instructor David Berman to speak at outside conferences, directs business Peters' way, and helps plug the ipicd's annual conference in Las Vegas, where past presenters have included Taser-backed researchers and employees. A flyer for . . . October [2008]'s three-day shindig, which drew 250 attendees, promised the "historic" opportunity to help form a "general consensus about excited delirium that will then be published in leading medical, legal, and law enforcement journals." As an expert witness for Taser, Peters charges $5,000 plus $2,750 per day; in 2007, he was paid about $42,000.

Taser's Conflict of Interest

Peters sees nothing inappropriate about his Taser connections. "We are not aligned with them at all," he says, although "we did not distinguish ourselves enough" at the start. (Brave, now listed as an inactive director, says he remains a legal adviser at ipicd.) In any case, the institute will continue in its quest to entrench ED as a medical and psychological diagnosis, Peters says, "to quiet these folks" who don't believe it exists.

These folks include Heston attorney John Burton, who, not surprisingly, finds the ipicd/Taser bond problematic. "These guys want to help the police stop killing people, and they're trying to build a liability defense for when they do," he says. "The two things are in direct conflict."

Brave, for his part, has nothing but contempt for the company's critics. "How much more damage are we going to do to police officers by continuing to put forth this ignorant rhetoric?" he asks. "A druggie's mommy hires a plaintiff's attorney, and now we need to blame someone. Do we blame the person who sold them the drugs or the mommy who let them take the drugs or the kid who actually took the drugs? No. We blame the police and Taser, because they were present at the time of death."

5

Excited Delirium Is a Documented Phenomenon

US Department of Justice

The United States Department of Justice is the federal executive department responsible for the enforcement of the law and administration of justice.

Tasers are not risk free but are not high risk either. Use on individuals in water or on a slope may result in death because of these special circumstances, but Tasers do not pose a significant risk for cardiac dysrhythmia or lasting difficulty in breathing or pose a greater threat than other factors in subdual. However, any kind of subdual involving an individual with excited delirium has a high risk of mortality. Excited delirium involves a number of symptoms, such as psychosis, agitation, combativeness, and elevated body temperature, which may itself cause death. Risks of continued or repeated use of a Taser are unknown and such use may not subdue someone in a state of excited delirium.

Although exposure to CEDs [conducted energy device] is not risk free, there is no conclusive medical evidence within the state of current research that indicates a high risk of serious injury or death from the direct effects of CED exposure. Field experience with CED use indicates that exposure is safe in the vast majority of cases. Therefore, law enforcement need not refrain from deploying CEDs, provided the devices are used in accordance with accepted national guidelines. . . .

US Department of Justice, "Findings: Study of Deaths Following Electro Muscular Disruption: Interim Report," June 2008. www.ncjrs.gov. Copyright © 2008 by National Institute of Justice (NIJ). All rights reserved. Reproduced by permission.

The potential for moderate or severe injury related to CED exposure is low. However, darts may cause puncture wounds or burns. Puncture wounds to an eye by a barbed dart could lead to a loss of vision in the affected eye. Head injuries or fractures resulting from falls due to muscle incapacitation may occur.

CEDs can produce secondary or indirect effects that may result in death. Examples include deploying a device against a person who is in water, resulting in drowning, or against a person on a steep slope resulting in a fall, or ignition risk resulting from deployment near flammable materials such as gasoline, explosives or flammable pepper spray that may be ignited by a spark from a device.

Research shows that human subjects maintain the ability to breathe during exposure to CED.

There is currently no medical evidence that CEDs pose a significant risk for induced cardiac dysrhythmia when deployed reasonably. Research suggests that factors such as thin stature and dart placement in the chest may lower the safety margin for cardiac dysrhythmia. There is no medical evidence to suggest that exposure to a CED produces sufficient metabolic or physiologic effects to produce abnormal cardiac rhythms in normal, healthy adults.

Research shows that human subjects maintain the ability to breathe during exposure to CED. Although there is evidence of hyperventilation in human subjects immediately following CED exposure, there is no medical evidence of lasting changes in respiratory function in human subjects following exposure to CED.

CED technology may be a contributor to "stress" when stress is an issue related to cause of death determination. All aspects of an altercation (including verbal altercation, physical struggle or physical restraint) constitute stress that may represent a heightened risk in individuals who have pre-existing cardiac or other significant disease. Current medical research suggests that CED deployment is not a stress of a magnitude that separates it from the other components of subdual.

Excited Delirium

Excited delirium is one of several terms that describe a syndrome characterized by psychosis and agitation and may be caused by several underlying conditions. It is frequently associated with combativeness and elevated body temperature. In some of these cases, the individual is medically unstable and in a rapidly declining state that has a high risk of mortality in the short term even with medical intervention or in the absence of CED deployment or other types of subdual.

Excited delirium that requires subdual carries with it a high risk of death, regardless of the method of subdual. Current human research suggests that the use of CED is not a life-threatening stressor in cases of excited delirium beyond the generalized stress of the underlying condition or appropriate subdual.

In many cases of excited delirium, high body temperature is the primary mechanism of death. There is no medical evidence that exposure to CED has an effect on body temperature.

It [excited delirium] is frequently associated with combativeness and elevated body temperature.

The purported safety margins of CED deployment on normal healthy adults may not be applicable in small children, those with diseased hearts, the elderly, those who are pregnant and other at-risk individuals. The effects of CED exposure in these populations are not clearly understood and more data are needed. The use of a CED against these populations (when recognized) should be avoided but may be necessary if the situation excludes other reasonable options.

Studies examining the effects of extended exposure in humans to CED are very limited. Preliminary review of deaths following CED exposure indicates that many are associated with continuous or repeated discharge of the CED. The repeated or continuous exposure of CED to an actively resisting individual may not achieve compliance, especially when the individual may be under drug intoxication or in a state of excited delirium. The medical risks of repeated or continuous CED exposure are unknown and the role of CEDs in causing death is unclear in these cases. There may be circumstances in which repeated or continuous exposure is required but law enforcement should be aware that the associated risks are unknown. Therefore, caution is urged in using multiple activations of CED as a means to accomplish subdual.

All CED use should conform to agency policies. The decision to use a CED or another force option is best left to the tactical judgment of trained law enforcement at the scene.

6

Tasers Are Frequently Overused

Stephen D

Stephen D is a contributor to the Daily Kos.

Tasers are primarily unsafe because they are often improperly deployed. Law enforcement has deployed them on individuals who formed no threat to themselves or others. Systematically, Tasers are overused and this phenomenon is about more than a few bad police officers misbehaving. Likewise, Tasers are generally used when no weapon is needed, and have been used on children, the elderly, and those with disabilities. Tasers are unsafe because law enforcement uses them unsafely, leading to widespread abuse.

Over the past decade I and many others have blogged about individual cases where tasers have been abused by law enforcement agencies and individual law enforcement officials. From the Baron Pikes case where a young black man in custody was tased to death by a white police officer in a small town in Louisiana until he died to the increase in taser use in Chicago to the tasing of a a bedridden 86 year old grandmother in El Reno, Oklahoma, to the man tased while having a diabetic seizure—well you get the point. There's a vast number of such stories where tasers were used in situations for which they were not intended, but few comprehensive studies to support the claims by activists that taser abuse by law enforcement in America is widespread.

Stephen D, "ACLU Study: Arizona Cops Routinely Misuse and Abuse Tasers," *Daily Kos*, June 30, 2011. www.dailykos.com. Copyright © 2011 by *Daily Kos*. All rights reserved. Reproduced by permission.

For that reason, I'm gratified to learn that the ACLU [American Civil Liberties Union] in Arizona took it upon themselves to fund a study to determine whether tasers are being systematically abused by Arizona law enforcement agencies. The results of that study should not surprise anyone. From the Executive Summary:

> Many U.S. law enforcement and correctional agencies in the United States are using Tasers today. In Arizona, where TASER International has its corporate headquarters, the American Civil Liberties Union (ACLU) of Arizona asked large police departments and sheriff's offices about the number and percentage of officers armed with a Taser; virtually every sworn officer is provided with one.
>
> . . . However, all too often, Tasers are used *"preemptively" against citizens that do not present an imminent safety threat,* and even *offensively as a pain compliance tool.* What's more, both TASER International training materials and agency policies *anticipate that officers will use the weapon as a pain compliance tool.*

Tasers Are Systematically Overused

This study confirms what many of us have been saying for years: that tasers are not merely used as an alternative to lethal force. Far from it. Indeed, their primary use in many cases is simply to coerce and intimidate individuals who pose no danger of imminent harm. The number of reports of taser misuse are not simply the result of "liberal bias." The abuse of tasers by law enforcement officials is not merely the result of a few bad apples or rogue cops. As the ACLU in Arizona has documented, the use of tasers to compel compliance and even torture people already in custody is not a bug, it's a feature. It's right there in the instructional materials provided by Taser International, and, at least in Arizona (though I'm quite sure this is the case in many other states as well) in the policies for using tasers adopted by many law enforcement agencies.

Here's some other relevant findings by the ACLU:

> One of the most striking and more significant findings that came out of the ACLU of Arizona's study is that, contrary to claims by Taser proponents, *the frequency of deployment of lethal force has not declined* with the advent of Tasers. [. . .]

> [T]he ACLU's survey of Arizona law enforcement agencies revealed that jurisdictions have adopted a patchwork of *inconsistent policies* regarding the Tasing of pregnant, young or elderly suspects, use of Tasers near a flammable substance, using Tasers on intoxicated people, and deploying the Taser multiple times on an individual. [. . .]

> . . . Amnesty International's recent 127-page report highlighting deaths associated with Taser use found that *the county in the United States with the highest number of reported deaths* was Arizona's own *Maricopa County.*

[T]asers have not lowered the rate at which deadly force is employed, despite Taser International's claims to the contrary.

Tasers Are Routinely Deployed

As the ACLU makes clear, Taser International has always touted that tasers are a safe and effective alternative to lethal force. What Taser International fails to mention, however, is that tasers are most often used in situations where lethal force is not necessary or warranted. Let me quote the study again:

> [T]he reality is that the majority of Taser shocks fired by officers do not take the place of gunshots, but rather other, less-lethal uses of force, such as baton strikes, chemical sprays, and the like. As the ACLU of Arizona's law enforcement survey suggests, *Tasers are routinely deployed in situations where lethal force would not be justified* (i.e., in the absence of an immediate threat to officer or public safety.) [. . .]

In a 2004 special report, The Arizona Republic analyzed use-of-force reports from the Phoenix Police Department for 377 incidents involving a Taser and found that *in nearly nine of of 10 cases, the subjects had not threatened officers with any weapon before a Taser was used.*

In short, tasers have not lowered the rate at which deadly force is employed, despite Taser International's claims to the contrary. What they have done is to increase the use of an often deadly device to coerce people to comply with the police in situations where there is no danger of any threat to the officers or to the public. Tasers have been employed against diabetics, people with epilepsy, people with heart conditions, the elderly, children and even pregnant women. They have been used against people already handcuffed and in custody. For all too many law enforcement officials they provide a lazy way to deal with people with whom those officers come into contact.

Taser Abuse Is Widespread

And to be fair, this isn't a problem only in Arizona. The ACLU cites the following 2007 report by the *Houston Chronicle* as further evidence that Taser abuse and misuse is widespread in other communities across the United States:

> In Houston, for example, a 2007 investigation revealed that in *95 percent of more than 1,000 incidents* over two years, Tasers were *"not used to defuse situations in which suspects wielded weapons and deadly force clearly would have been justified."* In approximately *35 percent of the cases examined* by the Houston Chronicle, *no crime was committed* at all. And of those people charged with crimes, *most were accused of misdemeanors or nonviolent offenses.*

Taser abuse is rampant. The statistics in Arizona clearly document that this is the case in at least one state. It would be easy to bash Arizona, but we know from the studies that have been done in Houston and Chicago, and the other, numerous local news reports that incidents of taser abuse by the police occur all across the country. As Annie Lai, staff attorney for the Arizona ACLU, and a co-author of the report succinctly put it:

> *"In many cases, you find that officers go for the Taser as the first instinct, rather than being trained in situations to de-escalate a situation or using alternative, less-severe uses of force."*

A cop armed with a taser doesn't have to put up with any lip from anyone.

Tasers Are Used Carelessly

That's the problem in a nutshell. If you are a police officer, why try to resolve a situation peacefully, or use a less lethal method to deal with individuals who do not immediately comply with what you tell them to do, when you have your trusty taser right there on your hip, ready to pull out and shock non-violent offenders or simply innocent individuals who pose no threat to you or anyone else. It's a lot easier to use a taser rather than deal with the "hassle" of keeping the "peace" by using less violent means. Thus, we end up with police using tasers indiscriminately against almost anyone who looks at them cross-eyed, or (in the case of some sick and sadistic cops) as a means to torture individuals already safely in custody. In situations in which officers would never think to use a firearm, they are more than willing to use a taser.

A cop armed with a taser doesn't have to put up with any lip from anyone. Even a routine traffic stop can end with you being shocked multiple times if he or she is in a bad mood, or you fail to comply fast enough with the cop's demands. The taser encourages violence against ordinary citizens by the police, rather than discourages it. And in all too many cases it kills people. People like Baron Pikes whom I mentioned above.

Yet, where is the outcry in the national media about this epidemic of police abuse and excessive force? Nowhere to be found. I guess we will just have to wait until some celebrity or pretty blonde young woman from a good family suffers death by taser before the national media will stand up and take notice.

In the meantime, the widespread use of tasers is eroding the public's trust in their law enforcement officials. I know that I always get anxious when I come across a police officer these days. He or she may be a dedicated and helpful public servant who plays by the rules, but how can you or I know for certain. We can't, and that's the real tragedy the ACLU has documented and wants to solve. Yet without coverage by the media of this problem leading to public outrage and a demand to deal with these issues, it's unlikely that individual states or Congress will do anything to stop what happens all to often to many, many people in the United States of America: torture, and far too often death, by taser wielding cops.

7

Proper Training Will Prevent Taser Overuse

The National Institute of Justice (NIJ)

The National Institute of Justice (NIJ) is the research, development, and evaluation agency of the US Department of Justice, and is dedicated to improving knowledge and understanding of crime and justice issues through science.

Since Tasers became more popular during the late 1990s, a number of problems have ensued. Because the use of Tasers by law enforcement has led to injuries and deaths, US citizens have questioned the use of stun gun technology. New technologies frequently raise questions when they are first deployed and Tasers are no different. In an attempt to better understand Taser use in everyday situations, the NIJ studied the use of conducted energy devices (CEDs) in the field. While Tasers have helped minimize physical struggles with suspects, law enforcement policies have sometimes failed to provide clear rules on Taser deployment and use. Because of this, some police officers rely on Tasers, even when no weapon is needed. At other times, police have overused Tasers, repeatedly shocking a suspect. Tasers, when used properly, are safe. It is important, however, for police departments to conduct training and create clear guidelines for Taser use.

This study looked at injuries that occur to law enforcement officers and citizens during use-of-force events. Most applications of force are minimal, with officers using their hands,

National Institute of Justice, "Police Use of Force, Tasers and Other Non-Lethal Weapons," NCJRS.gov, May 2011. Copyright © 2011 by National Institute of Justice. All rights reserved. Reproduced by permission.

arms or bodies to push or pull against a suspect to gain control. Officers are also trained to use various other force techniques and weapons to overcome resistance. These include less-lethal weapons such as pepper spray, batons or conducted energy devices (CEDs) such as Tasers. They can also use firearms to defend themselves or others against threats of death or serious bodily injuries.

> When police in a democracy use force and injury results . . . lawsuits often follow and the reputation of the police is threatened.

What Did the Researchers Find?

This study found that when officers used force, injury rates to citizens ranged from 17 to 64 percent, depending on the agency, while officer injury rates ranged from 10 to 20 percent. Most injuries involve minor bruises, strains and abrasions.

The study's most significant finding is that, while results were not uniform across all agencies, the use of pepper spray and CEDs can significantly reduce injuries to suspects and the use of CEDs can decrease injuries to officers.

The researchers assert that all injuries must be taken seriously. When police in a democracy use force and injury results, concern about police abuse arises, lawsuits often follow and the reputation of the police is threatened. Injuries also cost money in medical bills for indigent suspects, workers' compensation claims for injured officers or damages paid out in legal settlements or judgments. . . .

New Technologies Raise Questions

Police weaponry has come full circle.

During the middle of the 19th century, police officers in New York and Boston relied on less-lethal weapons, mostly wooden clubs. By late in the century, police departments began issuing firearms to officers in response to better armed criminals. Although firearms are still standard issue, law enforcement agencies are again stressing the use of less-lethal weapons rather than firearms.

The Fourth Amendment forbids unreasonable searches and seizures, and various other legal and policy controls govern how and when officers can use force. Most agencies tightly control the use of force and supervisors or internal affairs units routinely review serious incidents. New technologies have added to the concerns about the use of force by law enforcement.

During the past 20 years, new technologies have emerged that offer the promise of more effective control over resistive suspects with fewer or less serious injuries. Pepper spray was among the first of these newer less-lethal weapons to achieve widespread adoption by police forces, and more recently, conducted energy devices (CEDs) such as the Taser have become popular.

Taser use has increased in recent years. More than 15,000 law enforcement and military agencies use them. Tasers have caused controversy (as did pepper spray) and have been associated with in-custody deaths and allegations of overuse and intentional abuse. Organizations such as Amnesty International and the American Civil Liberties Union have questioned whether Tasers can be used safely, and what role their use plays in injuries and in-custody deaths.

[M]ost CED shocks produce no serious injuries.

Using Tasers

CEDs such as Tasers produce 50,000 volts of electricity. The electricity stuns and temporarily disables people by causing involuntary muscle contractions. This makes people easier to arrest or subdue. When CEDs cause involuntary muscle contractions, the contractions cause people to fall. Some people have experienced serious head injuries or bone breaks from the falls, and at least six deaths have occurred because of head injuries suffered during falls following CED exposure. More than 200 Americans have died after being shocked by Tasers. Some were normal, healthy adults; others were chemically dependent or had heart disease or mental illness.

Tasers use compressed nitrogen to fire two barbed probes (which are sometimes called darts) at suspects. Electricity travels along thin wires attached to the probes. (A new wireless Taser is also on the market.) Darts may cause puncture wounds or burns. A puncture wound to the eye could cause blindness.

Despite the dangers, most CED shocks produce no serious injuries. A study by Wake Forest University researchers found that 99.7 percent of people who were shocked by CEDs suffered no injuries or minor injuries only. A small number suffered significant and potentially lethal injuries.

This NIJ-sponsored study included six police departments and evaluated the results of 962 "real world" CED uses. Skin punctures from CED probes were common, accounting for 83 percent of mild injuries.

Policymakers and law enforcement officials want to know whether Tasers are safe and effective, and how (if at all) they should be used to match police use-of-force choices with levels of suspect resistance. This study indicates that CED use actually decreases the likelihood of suspect injury. . . .

Minimizing Physical Struggles

People rarely die after being pepper sprayed or shocked with a Taser. However, if injury reduction is the primary goal, agencies that allow use of these less-lethal weapons are clearly at an advantage. Both weapons prevent or minimize the physical struggles that are likely to injure officers and suspects alike.

Although both cause pain, they reduce injuries, and according to current medical research, death or serious harm associated with their use is rare. In that sense, both are safe and similarly effective at reducing injuries. Both should be allowed as possible responses to defensive or higher levels of suspect resistance. This recommendation is supported by the findings and is now followed by most agencies that responded to the national survey.

Deaths associated with CED use often involve multiple Taser activations (more than one Taser at a time) or multiple five-second cycles from a single Taser.

Taser Policy and Training Issues

CEDs were used far more often (four to five times more often) than pepper spray among agencies that equipped officers with CEDs and were sometimes used at rates that exceeded empty-hand control. Unlike pepper spray, CEDs do not require decontamination and do not carry the risk of accidental "blow back" that often occurs with pepper spray use. However, they do entail the removal of prongs and the potential for an unintended shock to an officer. Even with these concerns, they are rapidly overtaking other force alternatives. Although the injury findings suggest that substituting CEDs for physical control tactics may be useful, their ease of use and popularity among officers raise the specter of overuse.

The possible overuse of CEDs has several dimensions. CEDs can be used inappropriately at low levels of suspect resistance. Law enforcement executives can manage this problem with policies, training, monitoring and accountability systems that provide clear guidance (and consequences) to officers regarding when and under what circumstances CEDs should be used, or when they should not be used.

Besides setting the resistance threshold appropriately, good policies and training would require that officers evaluate the age, size, gender, apparent physical capabilities and health concerns of a suspect. In addition, policies and training should prohibit CED use in the presence of flammable liquids or in circumstances where falling would pose unreasonable risks to the suspect (in elevated areas, adjacent to traffic, etc.). Policies and training should address the use of CEDs on suspects who are controlled (e.g., handcuffed or otherwise restrained) and should either prohibit such use outright or limit them to clearly defined, aggravated circumstances.

In addition to being used too often, CEDs can be used too much. Deaths associated with CED use often involve multiple Taser activations (more than one Taser at a time) or multiple five-second cycles from a single Taser. CED policies should require officers to assess continued resistance after each standard cycle and should limit use to no more than three standard cycles. Following CED deployment, the suspect should be carefully observed for signs of distress and should be medically evaluated at the earliest opportunity.

Directions for Future Taser Research

CEDs can be used too much and too often. A critical research question focuses on the possibility of officers becoming too reliant on CEDs. During interviews with officers and trainers, the researchers heard comments that hinted at a "lazy cop" syndrome. Some officers may turn to a CED too early in an encounter and may relying on a CED rather than rely on the officer's conflict resolution skills or even necessary hands-on applications. Research should explore how officers who have CEDs perceive threats, compared to officers who do not have them. In addition, it is important to determine when, during an encounter, an officer deploys the CED.

Another important CED-related research project would be a case study of in-custody deaths involving CED use and a matched sample of in-custody deaths when no CED use occurred. Advocacy groups argue that CEDs can cause or contribute to suspect deaths. The subjects in CED experimental settings have all been healthy people in relatively good physical condition who are not under the influence of alcohol or drugs. There is no ethical way to expose overweight suspects who have been fighting or using drugs to the effects of CEDs, so an examination of cases where similar subjects lived and died may shed some light on the reasons for the deaths. Law enforcement officials typically argue that most if not all the subjects who died when shocked by a CED would have died if the officers had controlled and arrested them in a more traditional hands-on fight. At this point, the argument is rhetorical and research is needed to understand the differences and similarities in cases where suspects died in police custody, including deaths where a CED may or may not have been involved.

8

David Rosman: Second Amendment Calls into Question Columbia's Prop 2

David Rosman

David Rosman is an award winning editor, writer, and college instructor.

[Editor's note: In 2010, Proposition 2 considered the use of Tasers in Columbia, Missouri. If the proposition had been approved, it would have outlawed the use of Tasers by law enforcement and residents in Columbia. The proposition was defeated, with 77% of voters in Columbia voting against the measure.] Tasers have helped reduce injuries to suspects during altercations with law enforcement, and the citizens of Columbia should vote against Proposition 2. Likewise, outlawing the use of Tasers by citizens is the equivalent of outlawing guns, which are a guaranteed right under the US Constitution. Owning Tasers, like guns, should be a right.

> A well regulated Militia, being necessary to the security of a free State, the right of the people to keep and bear Arms, shall not be infringed.
>
> *—The Second Amendment to the U.S. Constitution*

This is about Tasers, the Second Amendment and your vote on Nov. 2. Proposition 2 would ban the use of a Taser, stun gun or other electrical device by anyone, including the police. An offender would be charged with a misdemeanor. Dan Claxton's recent report asked, in part, if the Taser is an "arm" as defined by the Second Amendment. The answer made our "right to bear arms" a more complicated argument than most contemplate.

I will be voting "no" on Proposition 2. I see the Taser as a tool that has reduced injuries to police officers and suspects. Yes, the Taser has been associated with injury and death, but so have batons. And for that matter, so have butter knives.

In my mind, the Second Amendment argument may be an English 101 problem, a question of definitions and grammar.

"Militia"—citizen soldiers. In the late 1700s, the militia was the citizen army sanctioned by the state and included all free men, or the "people." Today our volunteer civilian Army is the National Guard. Militia does not mean the wackos deep in the forests, hiding their activities, and working contrary to the interests of the state.

"Arms"—Weapons. The Founders had single-shot pistols, hunting rifles and shotguns, the standard issue of the day to bring food to the table. Today, we have redefined "Arms" to include semi- and full-automatic firearms as well as the Taser. Proposition 2 would prevent a civilian from using a Taser for self-protection but would allow that person to use a pistol. What is wrong with this picture?

Further complicating the discussion it appears that people on both sides of the argument forget one small section, "being necessary to the security of a free State." The Second Amendment allows for the citizen soldiers, "the public," to "keep and bear Arms" to protect the state and its citizens. In 1774 through 1787, the citizen soldier brought his own rifle. Today, though you can buy a civilian version of the M-14, the citizen soldier's arms are supplied by the state.

Note, the amendment does not say "own Arms," something today's proponents and opponents fail to mention in their collective discussions. My argument is that if the arms are distributed by the military or sanctioned paramilitary organization, its members should be able to keep and bear those weapons for the defense of the country and citizens. Did the Founders mean "own, keep and bear arms"? If they did, why didn't they write that?

Let's get back to Proposition 2. Prop 2 would make it a "Class A misdemeanor for individuals, including police officers, to use or threaten to use Tasers, stun guns or any other conducted electrical device against any person within the City." The proposal includes civilians who want a Taser or stun-gun for self-protection and extends to sheriff's deputies and state troopers.

We generally agree that a Taser is a weapon. If we also agree that police and other government-sanctioned paramilitary and public-safety organizations provide this weapon to its members in the name of public safety, then the banning of the use of Tasers would appear to be contrary to the Second Amendment.

We should never allow the NRA, the ACLU or any other group to put fear in our hearts when it comes to making a moral and legal decision . . . .

This issue will not stop with the Nov. 2 vote. The NRA and the ACLU, along with Taser-Free Columbia, will continue to battle, filling the airways and cyberspace with their sometimes zealot messages. "Chaos will take over the world if we . . ." One side screams, "Ban Tasers," while the other screams, "Allow Tasers."

We should never allow the NRA, the ACLU or any other group to put fear in our hearts when it comes to making a moral and legal decision like our vote on Proposition 2.

For me, "No" on Prop 2 is the right call, with all due respect to the fears and anxieties raised by the folks with Taser-Free Columbia. In this case, fears do not outweigh the Constitution.

9

Letter: Second Amendment Does Not Protect Taser Use

Ed Berg

Ed Berg lives in Columbia, Missouri.

[Editor's note: In 2010, Proposition 2 considered the use of Tasers in Columbia, Missouri. If the proposition had been approved, it would have outlawed the use of Tasers by law enforcement and residents in Columbia. The proposition was defeated, with 77% of the vote in Columbia against the measure.] Proposition 2 will not outlaw the use of Tasers, only the irresponsible use of Tasers. Likewise, the Second Amendment argument in relation to Tasers is incorrectly applied. First, the Supreme Court allows weapons to be regulated. Second, even the US Bureau of Alcohol, Tobacco, Firearms, and Explosives does not consider a Taser a firearm, so the people of Columbia should not be allowed to use Tasers indiscriminately.

David Rosman's October 25 column arguing against voting YES on the Prop 2 Taser initiative clearly shows a lack of understanding of the right given to citizens under the Second Amendment.

That right encompasses owning and possessing firearms. Prop 2 addresses only the use of the Taser. It places no restrictions on the right of a person to possess or to carry a Taser.

The Second Amendment and the right of possession of a firearm was defined clearly in the Supreme Court decision of

Ed Berg, "Second Amendment Does Not Protect Taser Use," *Columbia Missourian*, October 28, 2010. www.columbiamissourian.com. Copyright © 2010 by *Columbia Missourian*. All rights reserved. Reproduced by permission.

District of Columbia v. Heller in 2008. The majority opinion, written by Justice Scalia, scrutinized every word and phrase contained in the Second Amendment and concluded the Second Amendment guarantees citizens the right to possess firearms that might be used for self-defense, and this right shall not be tied to service in the militia.

Prop 2 ... places no restrictions on the right of a person to possess or to carry a Taser.

Further, the court found that there were limited restrictions that could be placed on the rights of certain persons to own or possess a firearm, e.g. convicted felons, the insane, or those under age. The court further found that the government had the power to restrict the use of firearms. This explains how we can have, within our city limits, specific restrictions in the form of municipal laws that limit certain uses of firearms, e.g. shooting off guns to celebrate New Year's or taking target practice in crowded areas.

In the *District of Columbia v. Heller* opinion, the court repeatedly used the term "firearms" when discussing the Second Amendment. The court went on to explain that although when the Second Amendment was ratified the citizens of the United States used the musket, the term "arms" contained in the Second Amendment applies to modern firearms now in common use.

Nowhere in the opinion is there any mention that arms also meant electric control devices such as the Taser.

Thus, the U.S. Supreme Court has found and specified that the term "to keep and bear arms" means that a citizen has a right to own and possess a firearm. The court has never found that a citizen has the right to use a firearm irresponsibly, in a way that would threaten the safety of others. To the contrary, the Supreme Court has found that the government has the right to regulate the manner in which firearms are used and to punish citizens who violate such restrictions. The initiative assumes that citizens have the right to own Tasers.

Under Missouri law, the Taser is classified as a "dangerous instrument" under Section 556.061.9 RSMo, and as a "Deadly Weapon" under Section 556.061.8 RSMo. Taser International recognizes this fact on its website. As such, the Taser is classified as a weapon capable of causing death or other serious physical injury when fired. Due to these legal classifications, the Taser's use can be restricted.

Taser International developed the Taser so that it would not be classified a firearm. The Taser, instead of gunpowder, uses a compressed inert nitrogen gas cartridge to shoot the probes. The U.S. Bureau of Alcohol, Tobacco, Firearms, and Explosives, at the request of its manufacturer, has classified the Taser as not being a firearm. This makes it possible for persons to purchase and carry the Taser concealed without meeting the strict requirements imposed on owners of a firearm.

Finally, Missouri Law Section 563.031 provides that a citizen of Missouri has the right to use any weapon in self defense if a person believes he or she may be harmed or killed by another person, or if a person enters his or her home or vehicle without permission, or refuses to leave the residence or the vehicle.

Taser International developed the Taser so that it would not be classified a firearm.

As far as citizen use of Tasers or electric control devices, Prop 2 affects only irresponsible use of the Taser, as in pranks, initiation rituals, or other threatening, outrageous behavior.

It is the people's right to set the use of force used by our police. Vote yes on Prop 2.

10

Tasers Should Not Replace Firearms in All Police Situations

Rick Guilbault

Rick Guilbault is the vice president of training for Taser International.

Tasers have offered law enforcement an effective weapon that can prevent the loss of life in many situations. A Taser, however, is not a replacement for a firearm. In fact, unclear law enforcement policies have led to a great deal of confusion regarding when and when not to use a Taser. While the public may believe that a police officer can disarm a suspect who has a gun by using a Taser, doing so has the potential to place the officer in danger. A police officer should never attempt to use a Taser if the suspect is armed with a dangerous weapon such as a knife or firearm. It is important that police officers receive proper training in order to understand when a Taser will be most effective.

Some special interest groups and at least one Texas legislator believe that TASERs should be used only when deadly force is justified. This is a very dangerous philosophy. It not only shows ignorance regarding police use of force, it essentially negates the TASER's usefulness as a means of reducing officer and suspect injuries.

Even some of the strongest critics of police use of force would agree that limiting TASER use to deadly force situations is a bad idea. Nobody would mistake the American Civil Liberties Union [ACLU] for a pro-police organization, but the ACLU says that TASERs are not an appropriate response when facing a bad guy with a gun. "There is significant pressure in some segments of the community to put electronic control device use at or just below lethal force. [This is] naive [and] it gives officers a dangerous choice and will lead to more deaths," Scott Greenwood, general counsel to the National Board of the ACLU, said at a recent TASER symposium.

Confusion in the Ranks

Even the ACLU realizes that TASERs are not a substitute for guns. But some officers have become confused as to when to use a TASER and when to use their duty weapons. The old saying "Never bring a knife to a gunfight" applies just as well for a TASER. A TASER is a great less-lethal weapon, but it is not a replacement for a gun.

Most cops know this. So where does the confusion come from?

Perhaps it comes from the fact that the introduction of TASERs into police operations in a given community tends to result in a reduction in officer-involved shootings. When the Miami-Dade Police Department equipped its police officers with TASERs, there were no officer-involved shootings for 12 months. The same thing happened in Seattle. That hadn't happened in either city in a decade.

A Taser is a great less-lethal weapon, but it is not a replacement for a gun.

Neither of these agencies trained its officers to use TASERs when facing threats of death or serious bodily injury. So the reduction in officer-involved shootings is likely the result of officers using their TASERs to resolve dangerous situations quickly and decisively before they could escalate to the level of requiring deadly force. This includes apprehending subjects who are later found to be armed with a firearm. It also frequently includes situations involving suspects armed with edged weapons or dangerous impact weapons such as hammers and pipes.

Does this mean a threat from a knife or a hammer should be responded to by the police with a TASER? Of course not. But under certain circumstances, a TASER might be a reasonable and appropriate response.

Saving Lives

But let's be clear on one thing: Officers should not expose themselves to any greater risk when armed with a TASER than they would if they had no TASER. These weapons were created to reduce officer deaths and injuries, not to create circumstances that put officers at greater risk.

Still, TASERs can be and have been used to prevent unnecessary deaths. For example, by utilizing appropriate physical cover as well as cover from an officer prepared to immediately deliver deadly force, officers have been able to safely approach and incapacitate subjects armed with lethal weapons.

Consider that many veteran officers have experienced lengthy standoffs with subjects who are armed with anything from knives to guns to pipes. Sometimes they happen in the open with officers in very close proximity (often too close) to the subject but not close enough to effectively use a baton or pepper spray. The subject is armed and not cooperative, but he is not threatening the officers, yet. In circumstances like these, incapacitating the subject early in the encounter with a TASER from say 20 to 30 feet away could end the situation before it escalates any further. But if the subject suddenly charges the officers, they will have no choice but to use deadly force.

Public Perceptions

Part of the reason why some cops have come to believe that a TASER can be a suitable response to a deadly threat is that in their zeal to promote TASER use by their officers some police administrators have led the public to believe a TASER can replace a gun. Many chiefs and sheriffs have been quoted saying that being hit by a TASER is better than being hit by a bullet.

This is indisputably true, but it's also misleading. It gives the public the perception that officers will be able to routinely resolve deadly force situations with a TASER. A more appropriate statement might be, "Getting hit by a TASER is safer than being struck by a baton and more effective than a snoot full of OC [oleoresin capsicum or pepper spray]."

These weapons were created to reduce officer deaths and injuries, not to create circumstances that put officers at greater risk.

Misleading the public is a political problem. Giving officers the impression that a TASER can replace a handgun is a tactical problem, and one that can lead to black mourning tape on your agency's badges.

I occasionally receive e-mails from officers describing how they were able to use their TASERs to disarm subjects who were attacking them with edged weapons or even firearms. They are grateful that no one was hurt and that they didn't have to take a life.

While I am happy that everything ended well for them, I fear they are committing one of the cardinal sins of police work: confusing good luck with good tactics. I have followed up with these officers and expressed my concerns to them. More importantly, I have contacted the department trainers to discuss the issue and make sure their officers realize the limitations of these devices and don't think of it as a replacement for a firearm. Because TASERs are typically very effective when properly applied to a subject, these situations often end with a successful apprehension and no injuries. However, one missed probe or a clothing disconnect can result in tragedy.

Some have voiced concern that some of the actual use videos contained in the TASER International instructor training course promote poor tactics and the use of TASERs in deadly force situations. The company clearly informs instructors and students that just by showing the video, it is not supporting the tactics depicted. In fact, some of the videos are examples of what not to do and of what can go wrong in the field.

In my classes, these videos have initiated some spirited debates as to whether deadly force would have been a more appropriate force option. This is, in fact, the purpose behind these videos, to promote discussions and get instructors thinking about appropriate tactics and force options.

Policies and Tactics

Another reason that many officers are confused about when to use a TASER and when not to use a TASER is that there is no consensus on this issue among chiefs and sheriffs.

Use-of-force policies and tactics vary from agency to agency. What is appropriate use of force within a sheriff's department might be prohibited in a police department within the same county.

The key concern is that officers know the policy and know when to use their TASERs. I have seen policies that very clearly state that a TASER shall not be used when deadly force is justified or when dealing with anyone armed with a firearm.

While as a general rule this might not be a bad idea, policy makers should consider that just because deadly force is justified does not always make it the best option. We also know that officers are not automatically justified in using deadly force simply because someone is armed with a firearm. Officers should be able to evaluate each situation on its own merits and should have all their tools at their disposal.

11

Easily Available Tasers Can Be Used for Self-Defense and to Commit Crimes

Silja J.A. Talvi

Silja J.A. Talvi is an investigative journalist and the author of Women Behind Bars.

While a Taser is generally viewed as a weapon for law enforcement, American citizens are also allowed to own stun guns in most states. Because of this, Taser International has directly marketed new versions of its weapons to women as self-protection. "The Lady Taser" is a handheld stun gun that comes in multiple colors, and has been promoted by sellers at Tupperware-styled parties. While the aggressive marketing of the Lady Taser has been successful, it has also been based on the fear factor: the Lady Taser, the company promotes, can protect women from assault and rape. Tasers have also become well-known within popular culture, and a number of public deployments of Tasers have been well documented. The media have also romanticized the use of Tasers. Unfortunately, Tasers have been overused and have been deployed against helpless individuals. Worse still, Tasers are being used by criminals. Taser International, however, appears less concerned with the potential misuse of the weapons than in selling as many stun guns to women as possible.

The SUV-driving, stun-gun-wielding housewife is coming to a suburb near you. In Arizona, Tupperware-style Taser parties have become all the rage, thanks to the enterprising savvy of saleswoman Dana Shafman, founder of Shieldher Inc.

Shafman's little soirees aren't just popular, they're also highly profitable. Over light conversation and snacks, women are invited to handle the palm-sized C2, the latest (and smallest) civilian version of a Taser stun gun. The C2 is also the most affordable Taser to hit the market, starting at $299.99—with an option to upgrade the C2 with a $50 laser beam to better the chances of debilitating a human target. Because practice makes perfect, the women in attendance are encouraged to grab a C2 and take turns shooting at a cardboard cutout representing a male attacker.

"I felt that we have Tupperware parties and candle parties to protect our food and house, so why not have a Taser party to learn how to protect our lives and bodies?" Shafman told the the *Arizona Republic*. Shafman projects that the parties will be held in at least a half-dozen other states by March.

The C2 comes in four iPod-matching metallic colors: "Hot pink" has been the top seller since the weapon hit the consumer market last summer. While the company admits that men, too, might benefit from carrying the mini-stunner, Taser's marketing strategy has been directed at the phobic and fashion-forward female consumer.

The Lady Taser

Last July, *The New York Times* previewed the C2's debut with a feature article titled, "Feeling Secure With a Little Shocking Pink." Accompanying the article was a glamour-action photo of Taser International President Kathy Hanrahan with the weapon in hand. Hanrahan made no bones about the C2's direct marketing strategy and conceptual design: "It's a woman's product," she said.

In a number of promotional media appearances and technology conference presentations since that time, Taser officials have even gone so far as to dub the C2 the "Lady Taser."

"When you're going out to a nightclub or you have the device clipped onto your belt at a business meeting, you don't want to look like Dirty Harry," company spokesperson Steve Turtle told ABC News last summer.

In what could have easily passed as a terribly tacky infomercial, ABC News ran a December 2007 "Money Matters" segment praising the palm-sized stunner as an exciting holiday gift for women, in which anchor Laura Marquez described the C2 as a "Taser with a softened look."

Despite a plethora of headline-making news over the course of the year [in 2008]—including the notorious "Don't Tase Me, Bro" incident during Sen. John Kerry's (D-Mass.) University of Florida speech in September 2007—ABC News showcased Taser's own video montage of alleged male criminals being stunned into submission. For the ABC News segment, the network opted for a large-font text banner to accompany the images: "Tasers Sold to Protect Women."

None of those video snippets actually depicted women being attacked, and the network's Taser-friendly sloganeering (and Marquez's ridiculously soft-balled questions) didn't seem coincidental in the least.

The success of Taser's C2 sales . . . can largely be attributed to the company's aggressive strategy to play on women's worst fears . . . .

Taser's Aggressive Marketing

The Scottsdale, Ariz., corporation has spent years honing a relentless public relations campaign—complete with a Rolodex of at-the-ready medical, legal and law enforcement stun technology "experts"—that seems to have convinced many news outlets that Taser's word is gospel truth.

The success of Taser's C2 sales over the past several months can largely be attributed to the company's aggressive strategy to play on women's worst fears of assault and rape. While the C2 might look cute, it is utterly debilitating—a serious step up, as it were, from older self-defense products like mace and pepper spray.

Just as with the "professional" model, a triggered mini stun gun shoots out two, thin nitrogen-fueled wires with dart-like tips that penetrate clothing and embed in the skin. These darts are juiced to deliver an incapacitating 50,000 volts of electricity for 30 uninterrupted seconds—ostensibly to allow the Taser-wielder to make a quick getaway.

Aside from the various bells and whistles that would appeal to paramilitary-minded weapon owners, the key difference between C2s and the much more costly civilian and "professional" versions of X-26s is that they enable the "stunner" to shock the "stunnee" over and over again.

The Popularity of Tasers

Whether we're talking about cutesy mini-stunners, or their beefed-up big brothers, Taser has become a household name and a veritable pop culture phenomenon rooted in either opposition or celebration of this futuristic weapon that was once but a gleam in [science fiction writer] Gene Roddenberry's creative eye. (Unlike the Taser, the sci-fi *Star Trek* "phaser" could specifically be set to a specific stun level, all the way up to a deadly jolt.)

Devoted Trekkies with "Set Phasers to Stun!" T-shirts were likely never the cool kids on the block, but "Don't Tase Me, Bro" bumper stickers and T-shirts are a different story. Some are wearing the shirts to express their outrage toward the prevalence of Tasers in use by "campus cops" on college, high school, middle school and even elementary school grounds—as well as in political demonstrations as a terrifying method of crowd control.

But you might be just as likely to spot a clean-cut fraternity member wearing the same shirt—only to find that he hasn't given a thought as to whether being hit repeatedly with 50,000 volts of electricity should be considered an act of torture.

There's been no shortage in the blogosphere of people poking fun of [Taser victim] Andrew Meyer's appeals, moans and screams that accompanied the University of Florida incident. Indeed, sites like www.dont-tasemebro.com are further proof of the ways in which even the most serious issue can be trivialized and depleted of its power. Why pass up a perfect opportunity to make a bit of money ($29.95 per T-shirt, to be exact) on a popular slogan, even if it originated in the pleading moments before the sickening crack-snap-sizzle sound of a Taser shooting electrified darts into a person's skin?

People who have been tased often liken the experience to the sensation of dying . . . .

Romanticizing Tasers

Taking outright pleasure in the pain the weapon can inflict, the popular TV series "24" seems to have developed a love affair with this kind of weaponry. At least two "terrorists" have been stun-gunned thus far, in addition to Abu Ghraib-style electrical torture during interrogations.

Even low-budget Asian martial arts movies shown in the United States feature the occasional stun gun stunt, alongside more familiar, high-flying punches and kicks.

People who have been tased often liken the experience to the sensation of dying—something that does not seem like an exaggeration in light of at least 250 Taser-related deaths in the United States since 2001, according to Amnesty International. The U.N. Committee Against Torture recently determined that the use of Tasers "causes acute pain, constituting a form of torture."

Until recently, reports of Taser-related incidents and deaths have tended to involve men, typically described by police as having behaved in deranged and/or dangerous ways before being stunned.

But what once amounted to a few reported Taser encounters per month has now taken the shape of *daily* accounts throughout North America, including several high-profile deaths in Canada.

[In] September [2007], the death of a non-English-speaking Polish immigrant at the hands of inexplicably aggressive, Taser-wielding Royal Canadian Mounted Police at the Vancouver Airport drew international outrage when a bystander's cell phone footage thwarted initial "official" efforts to downplay what had happened.

Overusing Tasers

Increasingly, people being stunned aren't just people with limited English-speaking skills; they're also children, teenagers, the elderly and the disabled. In fact, with astonishing frequency, police are using Tasers on women and girls.

In November 2007, for instance, Chicago police tased an 82-year-old woman with dementia.

[In] June [2007], a homeless woman died outside an Oklahoma City shelter after she was thrown on the ground, handcuffed by police and *then* tased while incapacitated.

In Green Cove Springs, Fla., the family of an agitated 56-year-old wheelchair-bound woman filed suit last February [2007] after watching police shock her 10 times in response to their request for assistance. Her death was ruled a homicide.

Ohio has become an unexpected epicenter of the use of Tasers against women and girls. [In] May [2007], Crystalynn Coker, a 17-year-old African-American student was tased in Monroe, Ohio, when she refused to back down from a racist verbal barrage by a fellow student and staged her own form of a one-person, nonviolent sit-in after her teacher ordered *her* out of the classroom. According to Coker and her family, a police officer was called in without any justifiable cause to physically remove her from the room. Once the officer pulled Coker from her chair, he handcuffed and tased her three times without any explanation before, during or after the attack.

In the town of Warren, Ohio, footage emerged in September 2007 of a policeman shocking 38-year-old Heidi Gill repeatedly. In the video, Gill is shown crawling, moaning and pleading desperately as she tries to get away from the apparently trigger-happy officer. Footage shows Officer Rich Kovach handcuffing and dragging Gill's body around during much of the ordeal, which is now under investigation.

Tasers have already begun to be used in robberies, domestic violence and hostage situations.

Indiscriminate Taser Use

One of the strangest overreactions involving Taser use occurred in, of all places, a Best Buy electronics store in Daytona Beach, Fla. Amid frenetic rush of pre-Christmas shoppers, 35-year-old yoga instructor Elizabeth Beeland had been waiting in line to purchase a CD player with her credit card. When her cell phone rang, Beeland stepped outside the store's noisy environment to have a brief conversation. Although she left both the CD player and credit card with the cashier, the clerk somehow concluded that Beeland might be using a stolen card, and called police officer Claudia Wright over to handle the situation. Beeland took umbrage at the accusation, and raised her voice. Wright threatened to arrest her if she didn't stop yelling. In what has become an increasingly familiar scenario—the rapid escalation from an initial encounter with a civilian, culminating with the infliction of horrendous pain, sometimes within just a few seconds—Wright opted to use her X-26 over any number of more logical alternatives. On the surveillance tape, Beeland is seen trying to back away from the

Taser-wielding cop, then falling to the floor in obvious pain after the stun gun wires pierced her flesh.

Worse yet, Tasers have already begun to be used in robberies, domestic violence and hostage situations.

Among other disturbing reports, a serial rapist in Modesto, Calif., kidnapped and brutally raped a 27-year-old woman in August 2006 after stunning her with a Taser.

For the sake of those schmooze, stun and sales parties, they might do well to keep this kind of information under a tightly sealed Tupperware lid.

12

Tasers Are Not Practical for Self-Defense

Nicola Griffith

Nicola Griffith is a native of Yorkshire, England, where she taught women's self-defense before discovering writing and moving to the United States.

Tasers are being sold to women at Tupperware-style parties where the stun gun is promoted as a shortcut to self-protection against sexual assault. Instead of buying Tasers, women need to learn basic self-defense. Tasers may be effective, but a woman's first line of self-defense is her own bravery.

There's been a lot of buzz in the press about women's Taser parties. (They're like Tupperware parties, but sell C2 Tasers instead of plastic tubs.)

These reports infuriate me.

Apparently, many women who go to these parties live in constant fear of violent sexual assault. And they believe that having a Taser will protect them. Perhaps they imagine a hooded stranger in their apartment or their parking lot. Perhaps they imagine that they will whip out the Taser, zap the bad guy, and a few minutes later watch as the cops march him off. Bloodless and neat. Her Taser is a "safety blanket," says Dana Shafman, the entrepreneur who started the parties; if she leaves the house without one she goes "into panic mode."

But it's not safety blankets that protect you. You do that.

Nicola Griffith, "Taser Buzz Kill," *Huff Post Living*, April 4, 2008. www.HuffingtonPost .com. Copyright © 2008 by Nicola Griffith. All rights reserved. Reproduced by permission.

The Limitations of Tasers

You start by being informed. Most (68%) violent and/or sexual assaults are perpetrated by a man the woman knows. Most assaults happen in or near the woman's home (72%) or the home of a neighbor or friend (11%). You are much more likely to get hurt in your breakfast nook than in a dark alley. The man trying to hurt you is more likely to be your ex-husband or boyfriend or colleague than a hooded stranger. So, statistically, we're talking about Tasing someone you know who moves on you unexpectedly in close quarters, in a place where you feel safe. But, hey, no problem, because the Taser is pretty foolproof. Right?

Well, no, not exactly.

The C2 Taser electroshock weapon, sold in a range of pretty colours (and designed to look like a woman's electric razor), is a one-shot-only device, effective to a maximum of 15 feet. If you miss with your one shot, you have to use the Taser as a contact stun gun (known as dry Tasing). Dry Tasing is not particularly effective for putting someone down; it hurts but doesn't incapacitate. You have to hold the weapon against your target for at least five seconds—and trust me, it's difficult to do anything for even two seconds in a fight.

Most (68%) violent and/or sexual assaults are perpetrated by a man the woman knows.

So don't miss with that first shot. But, hey, why would you? After all, it's easy to hit something as big as a man from 15 feet. Right?

Well, no, not exactly.

Maybe your assailant will announce politely from no more than 15' away that he wishes to hurt you, then stand still and wait patiently as you struggle to understand what's happening, remember where you put the Taser, pull it out, and aim. Maybe your hands won't be shaking from adrenaline.

Good. Then shoot him and put him down. Put the Taser on the floor next to him and walk away while, for 30 seconds (six times as long as the maximum used by police Tasers), the C2 pumps current into his nervous system. This could lead to permanent heart arrhythmias and/or fractured vertebrae. But why should you care? No doubt your assailant deserves it. There again, the person getting damaged could end up being you. Like any weapon, the Taser can be taken away and used against you. Remember all those stories you've read about home owners killed by their own guns? I see no reason to suppose that the statistics for Taser owners would be any different.

The Importance of Training

A weapon is only useful if you're willing and able to use it when you're attacked. So if you buy a Taser (or pepper spray, or gun), be prepared to carry it with you everywhere—the shower, the conference room, while taking out the garbage. Practice drawing it and firing it. Come up with all the what-if scenarios you can imagine, and rehearse them. A Taser isn't a magic amulet, able to protect you simply by existing. It's a tool (a moderately useless one, in my opinion), and it is as only as effective as the person using it.

A weapon is only useful if you're willing and able to use it when you're attacked.

The quote from a Taser buyer that disturbs me the most comes from an Arizona Taser party host. "If you know you're going to be in a certain situation where you might be uncomfortable, why not have it with you? It just makes you more confident."

And we're back with the notion of a safety blanket. But safety blankets have never saved anyone. Here's a better way to approach the possibility of danger: don't expect a weapon you haven't trained with for a hundred hours or more to function as a mystical shield. If you do, you'll be blunting your most powerful survival tool: your instincts. When you begin to feel uncomfortable in a situation—when you are afraid—that's your instincts, screaming at you that something is wrong. Those instincts can save your life. (Read Gavin de Becker's *The Gift of Fear.*) Don't smother them under a safety blanket.

I taught self-defense for five years in the UK. It works. According to U.S. Department of Justice statistics, women fight off unarmed rapists successfully 72% of the time. If he has a knife, she'll fight him off 58% of the time. If he has a gun, she has a 51% chance. Unarmed, untrained, if you fight back, you'll probably win. But if weapons make you feel better, then just look around you—they're everywhere. In your purse: perfume, nail file, phone. In your kitchen: cleaning spray, fire extinguisher, all those knives. In your car: air freshener, cigarette lighter, and the car itself.

The world, as [fictional female detective] Aud Torvingen would say, is a "garden of weaponry." Tasers are the least of these. The most important are the ones you always have with you: your mind, your common sense, your bravery. Your best weapon is yourself.

13

Tasers Should Not Be Marketed to Women

Marc H. Rudov

Marc H. Rudov is the author of The Man's No-Nonsense Guide to Women.

In recent years, laws have been passed that give women more rights than men. This has allowed women a number of advantages, including the right to accuse men of crimes such as rape. Even when suspects have been proven innocent, women are not held accountable for false accusations. Because of this, the idea of selling good Tasers to women is troublesome. In essence, a woman can now buy a Taser and, for no good reason, decide to use it on her husband or boyfriend with impunity. While there are a number of things a man might ask a woman he is becoming involved with, now there is a new question: Do you own a Taser?

In case you didn't know, October [2007] was "Domestic Violence Awareness Month," during which Americans were startled to learn that *women are just as likely as men to commit domestic violence.* Mention this at a party, and you'll find yourself standing alone at the punchbowl for the rest of the night: people just don't want to hear it. Sugar and spice, remember?

Because of VAWA (Violence Against Women Act), American men are *presumptively and, therefore, unconstitutionally* tagged as predators. Men must face a feminist justice system of proving innocence, instead of being protected by the US Constitution, which requires prosecutors to *prove guilt*. They have Senator Joseph Biden (D-DE) to thank for this—just ask the three exonerated lacrosse players from Duke University. And, what happened to Crystal Gail Mangum, the woman who was protected by an unconstitutional rape-shield law after she falsely accused them of rape? The same thing that happens to all fraudulent rape accusers: nothing. What do the feminist presidential candidates (Hillary *and* the men) have to say about this: nothing. How many of you men in Delaware will reelect Joe Biden?

The misandrist [anti-men] climate doesn't end there. Because of IMBRA [International Marriage Broker Regulation Act], the unconstitutional law that Senator Sam Brownback (R-KS) sponsored, American men are considered dangerous to foreign women. That's right, foreign women in foreign countries now have more American rights than American men living in America. Because of IMBRA, foreign women now have the power to demand unilateral background checks on American men before dating them. Worse, they can do whatever they want with this confidential information. How many of you men in Kansas will reelect Sam Brownback?

Men must face a feminist justice system of proving innocence, instead of being protected by the US Constitution. . . .

The Shocking Truth

Enter the "Taser for ladies," available in metallic pink for $350 from Taser International, Inc., in Scottsdale, AZ. A news item on Fox News described the latest fad: women having Taser parties, redolent of Tupperware parties, where they get each other to purchase these weapons. Do women sometimes find themselves in dangerous situations where they need protection? Absolutely. Because of VAWA, do women have the potential to fraudulently use Tasers, with impunity—in arguments, in rages, out of jealousy, for spite, in revenge, etc.—to commit legal assault and battery on innocent men? You bet they do!

A Taser purchaser must register with and get approval from the company. What about training, though? If she uses it, where on a man's body will she aim it? Is she liable for any harm to him? Is she obligated to get him medical attention? According to the company Website: TASER® energy weapons are not considered firearms—they're legal to carry in most states without permits (including California). They are restricted from citizen use in MA, RI, NY, NJ, WI, MI, HI, IL, and certain cities and counties. According to a German consultant to the company, Tasers, as consumer products, are currently illegal in Europe.

There are many things you might want to say during a romantic evening gone badly, but the last one is: "Don't tase me, babe!"

If Taser weapons are not considered firearms, what are they considered? This presents yet another challenge to our hypocritical, gynocratic "legal" system. I don't know what Tasers are considered, but I can guess: in the name of protecting women—translation: getting the female vote—our male legislators and judges will ignore the issue until men force them to deal with it. This is the shocking truth, folks.

Here's a scenario to ponder: If a maniacal wife attacks her husband, as so often happens, and he tases *her*, what do you suppose would happen to *him?* Ha! How many lawyers would it take to defend, to "prove his innocence"? Not to mention being pilloried by the media as a wimp (when a woman attacks a man, it is just emotion; let it go).

The No-Nonsense Bottom Line

I counsel every man to ask a new paramour, before becoming sexually involved with her, about: her use of birth control, her willingness to terminate an accidental pregnancy, and her carriage of [sexually transmitted diseases] STDs. Now, there is a new question to add: Do you own a Taser? If she does, and logic and perspective don't appear to be her strong suits, stay far, far away from her.

Remember Biden & Brownback: they have convinced their Senate and House colleagues to give women the preponderance of civil and criminal rights. They are responsible for creating the Department of Justice's unconstitutional Office on Violence Against Women. And, they will be responsible for women indiscriminately tasing men.

There are many things you might want to say during a romantic evening gone badly, but the last one is: "Don't tase me, babe!"

14

Tasers Should Not Be Used on Students

Pierre Tristam

Pierre Tristam is an editorial writer for the Daytona News-Journal, *focusing on the Middle East, foreign affairs, civil liberties, immigration, and federal politics.*

In an incident in Flagler Palm Coast High School in Florida, a special education student refused to complete his school work. When he became increasingly obstinate, the school teacher requested help. A police officer who worked within the school came to the classroom and asked the student to cooperate. When the student refused, the police officer attempted to pull the student from his desk. When the officer tried a second time, the student hit the officer with his palm. During the altercation, the officer removed his Taser and eventually used it to subdue the student. None of this should have happened. By dispatching the police officer, and by the police officer threatening the student, the student was provoked unnecessarily. The public should not remain indifferent to the incident, and Tasers should not be allowed in schools.

I'm not going to mention his name, even though it's been all over the media. His rights have been violated enough. So has his person, physically, violently, by the high school he attends, by the sheriff'ss deputy called to subdue him, and subsequently by the sheriff himself and the school district, who alternately rationalized, justified, excused and in some measures applauded what they should have condemned outright as a barbaric act: The willful electrocution by Taser of a 16-year-old boy, a special education student with emotional or behavioral problems, in his classroom, *for refusing to do his work*. They'll tell you that he hit a deputy. He did. But only in reaction to the deputy's attempt to wrestle the boy off his seat and forcibly remove him from his classroom *simply because the student refused to follow directions*. The whole thing unfolded in a matter of minutes, not hours: the school wanted to keep its schedule. By morning's end a 16-year-old had been booked at the county jail on a felony charge, then shipped off to a juvenile "detention" facility one county over. And the deputy typed "case closed" at the end of his incident report. This is the country we're living in, the police agencies we have to live with, and the school systems that enable them. This is the county *I'm* living in: this happened in my school district, in Flagler County, last Thursday, at Flagler Palm Coast High School, the school where my daughter would be attending in a couple of years, although I hear the former sheriff, speaking to the school board today, told the five men and women that "if this board doesn't take a stand you'll never get a chance to educate my 10-year-old child." Our daughter is being home-schooled in preparation for ninth grade there. But those words sound right to me.

An Everyday Incident

This, then, is what happened, based on what school district personnel said, what the sheriff said, and what the sheriff's incident report says. The student was in Robert Ripley's classroom. He was refusing to complete an assignment. He was being "disruptive." He was not being violent: he was not physically hurting anyone or anything. He was acting out. Nothing extraordinary there, in the sense that disruptions like that occur, even with "regular" students, and are expected to occur with special ed students. Paul Peacock, a vice-principal, and another individual whose name was misspelled on the incident report were in Robert Ripley's classroom when the "school resource deputy," Scott Vedder, arrived. (For those of you reading this in more civilized places, like New Jersey, cops are routinely assigned to permanent security detail in schools here, even in elementary schools, and euphemistically referred to as "school resource officers" or "school resource deputies." An uncle of mine from Princeton, N.J., who happened to be visiting here the evening after the incident at the high school, was describing to me a school in Jersey that was testing the law by attempting to forbid cops from entering school grounds even if going after a student suspect; the school was arguing that a school should be a sanctuary. Interesting idea. Heretical, in a semi-police state like Florida. Likely laughable, in a county like mine.)

Let Vedder's account in his incident report pick up the story at this point; the timeline picks up just before Vedder arrives, based on what the adults in the room told Vedder:

When [the student] was approached by his teacher R. Ripley, he became very belligerent and refused to participate. [The student] advised R. Ripley that he was not going to do the assignment and pushed all of his books onto the floor and threw his pencil across the room. At that time R. Ripley asked [the student] to leave the room with him. [The student] refused and said "f--- you." At that time Mr. Peacock walked into the class room [*sic*]. Upon Mr. Peacock being advised of the situation he had the other students relocate to the class room next door and asked for my assistance via school radio. While I was responding to the class room Mark Montieth arrived and he and Mr. Peacock continued to coax [the student] to leave the class room. [The student] refused to get out of his chair and go to the dean's office. I then attempted to talk with [the student]. I attempted to talk [the student] into leaving the class room peacefully. I

advised him that we needed to go to Mr. Peacock's office
and talk *before the situation gets worse than it needs to be.*

The emphasis is mine: not only has the deputy already escalated the situation by his presence; he is dropping threats of
how much further the situation *will* escalate. There's pre-
meditation in crime. There's also such a thing as pre-meditated
provocation, a police skill. You see it in action here: the student wasn't worsening the situation with his obstinacy. The
deputy was worsening it by forcing the issue. He had the student psychologically cornered and surrounded. Now he was
moving in, making the situation worse than it needed to be.
The incident report again:

> [The student] then advised that he was not getting up and
> nobody was going to get him out of the chair or the class
> room, Because [*sic.*] he did not want to go. I then advised
> [the student] that he did not have a choice in the matter,
> because *he was under arrest for disruption of a school func-
> tion.*

The emphasis is again mine. There's a new one on me.
You can get arrested for not doing your work. For not following a teacher's directions. For not going to "the office." It's a
wonder I didn't spend my entire elementary and middle school
career in prison. Then again I was attending school in a more
civilized place than this (by which I mean, of course, Leba-
non, where Jesuits had a more effective weapon than Tasers
and guns put together. It's called persuasion and patience, a
deadly combination if you're an obstinate student like me. Jesuits generally had intelligence on their side, too.) What
Deputy Scott Vedder promised, he fulfilled. It got worse:

> At that time I attempted to physically remove him from the
> desk with an escort technique of the right arm. [The stu-
> dent] immediately pulled his arm away and tensed up the
> muscles in his upper body resisting my attempt to remove
> him from the chair. I advised him that if he did not comply
> I would deploy my Taser.

Tasering a Student

An extremely important detain here: the deputy made his first threat of using the Taser *before* the student had acted violently. The school board and I suspect the majority of the public would—because of the way the sheriff's office conveyed the story—subsequently be under the impression that the Taser was used because the student struck the deputy. Not so. The deputy was ready to use the Taser whether or not the student was going to lift a hand to him, and makes that clear in the record.

> He again pulled his arm away from me, looked directly at me and pulled his drew his [*sic*] left hand back. [The student] then struck me in the left check with the palm of his left hand as I attempted to move out of his reach.

There's ... such a thing as pre-meditated provocation, a police skill.

At the school board meeting on Tuesday [February 6, 2007], the deputy's supervisor, Zane Kelly, exaggerated the situation just as he had exaggerated it when describing it to the press by saying that the student "struck my deputy with a closed fist." The incident report is clear: the deputy was struck "with the palm of [the student's] left hand." So it goes: not only do the authorities—school and police—needlessly escalate a situation, but the perceived gravity of the incident is needlessly escalated as it is subsequently described, and in a way that unequivocally demarcates victim from officer: the victim is a demon out of control; the officer is a hero who had no choice, and followed all protocols. They call these here, proudly, "the matrix of force." Here it is in action:

> At that time I disengaged from [the student] and drew my M26 Taser emitting the laser aiming function onto his chest and advised him several times to get down on the ground or I would deploy the Taser [*sic.*] [The student] refused to

~~comply so I then deployed the Taser by pulling the trigger~~ one time for a five second cycle. [That's 50,000 volts for five seconds, pronged into the student's skin.] [The student] then rolled off of the chair onto the ground. [The student] then complied with all of my commands and I was able to secure him without further incident.

Tasering a student in his school . . . is a greater crime than anything the student could have been doing.

If irony could speak. A important bit of history: Two years ago [in 2005] when the new sheriff was elected (Don Fleming who, incidentally, had been a police chief in a New Jersey Meadowlands town much like the one portrayed in "Copland") he immediately talked about arming his school cops with Tasers. The school board discussed it and rejected the idea. The sheriff said he'd comply. He was even quoted to that effect in the papers. Obviously, he didn't. The school board met on Tuesday [February 6, 2007]. The sense before the meeting was that a clear policy would be drawn up banning Tasers from schools. Not so fast. The board prevaricated. The board attorney advised against a policy, otherwise the school board would be liable should a student be hurt in an incident where, say, a gun was used where a Taser might have done better. So goes the twisted logic of agencies more fearful of lawsuits than protective of their students. No one seemingly condemned the use of the Taser outright. No one seemed, as they should have been, outraged. Doubt was getting more than its benefit. It was sprinkling the whitewash. So the best they could settle on was a workshop to discuss the matter further. Zane Kelly, the school cops' supervisor, even used the word "proud" when describing his deputy's reaction after the deputy was allegedly "struck." Because, Kelly said, the deputy backed up, composed himself, and ordered the student to comply.

Then he fired.

An Indifferent Public

And we wonder why we're living in such violent times. And we wonder why, when stories like this make it into the press, the reaction by the general public is revoltingly approving of the use of force under those false rationales that even the local superintendent and cops are quick to use: better a Taser than a gun. As if those were the only two options. As if we have become so barbaric in our algorithms of law and order that the only two variables in the formula *have* to be force and order. And all this because a 16-year-old boy, a special education student, was acting out. It reminds me of another recent incident in the Daytona Beach area a couple of weeks back [in February 2007] that began with a speeding car, was followed by a high-speed chase, and ended with thirty cops' bullets fired at the car. The two occupants somehow survived, though they were wounded. And the cops didn't even know if the person on the passenger side was a kidnapping victim or worse. But they fired. What triggered the folly in the student's case, and who's at fault for letting the student escalate to the point where a cop was in the classroom instead of a trained counselor, a conflict-resolution specialist, even a couple of medics for that matter? (The medics turned up later, post-zapping.)

The Palm Coast high school student is 275 pounds and 6 or 6-1. His size is used repeatedly as further justification that he could have been trouble. The more reason to invoke conflict-resolution techniques. His size, his age, his status as a special education student are all irrelevant in the end: Tasering a student in his school, in his classroom, a student who was causing no worse harm than upsetting, loudly and maybe aggravatingly, a day's routine, is a greater crime than anything the student could have been doing.

A couple of other details about the incident. The student is black. To my knowledge, every individual involved in his disciplining and cornering was white, even though the school has a black dean and a black assistant principal. Maybe color is irrelevant in this case. Maybe it isn't. It certainly shouldn't be ignored. Neither should this: The student's father died a violent death some years ago. And Tuesday [February 6, 2007], while the school board discussed his case in a cakewalk of prevarications, the student turned 17. Happy birthday. Oh, and this week is "Disability Awareness Week" at Flagler Palm Coast High School, "in order to create more compassion for those with disabilities." Great job.

Organizations to Contact

The editors have compiled the following list of organizations concerned with the issues debated in this book. The descriptions are derived from materials provided by the organizations. All have publications or information available for interested readers. The list was compiled on the date of publication of the present volume; the information provided here may change. Be aware that many organizations take several weeks or longer to respond to inquiries, so allow as much time as possible.

American Civil Liberties Union (ACLU)
125 Broad Street, 18th Floor, New York, NY   10004
(212) 549-2500
e-mail: wso@al-anon.org
website: www.aclu.org

The ACLU is a national organization that works to defend Americans' civil rights as guaranteed by the US Constitution. It has been a strong opponent of indiscriminate Taser use by law enforcement. Among the ACLU's numerous publications are the book *In Defense of American Liberties: A History of the ACLU*, the handbook *The Rights of Prisoners: A Comprehensive Guide to the Legal Rights of Prisoners Under Current Law*, and the briefing paper "Crime and Civil Liberties."

Amnesty International
1 Easton Street, London   WC1X 0DW
  UK
+44-20-74135500
website: www.amnesty.org

Amnesty International is a global movement of more than three million supporters, members, and activists in more than 150 countries and territories that campaign against human rights abuses. Its vision is for every person to enjoy all the rights enshrined in the Universal Declaration of Human Rights and other international human rights standards. Amnesty International is independent of any government, political ideology, economic interest, or religion. It publishes numerous reports and newsletters, available at its website.

The Association for Women's
Self Defense Advancement (AWSDA)
556 Route 17 North, Suite 7-209, Paramus, NJ 07652
(201) 794-2153 • fax: (201) 791-6005

The AWSDA is an international, nonprofit, educational organization, dedicated to ending violence against woman by providing training programs for instructors and services for women. AWSDA does not promote any specific self-defense type or style, but encourages training in various self-defense options ranging from empty handed self-defense to training in the use of lethal weapons.

Center for Safe Schools
275 Grandview Avenue, Suite 200, Camp Hill, PA 17011
(717) 763-1661
e-mail: safeschools@csc.csiu.org

Founded in 1995, Center for Safe Schools seeks to develop creative and effective solutions to problems that disrupt the educational process and affect school safety. The Center provides training and technical assistance to help schools identify and implement effective programs and practices and maintain safe, productive learning environments. The Center also serves as a state-wide clearinghouse for educators, parents, law enforcement, and others on school safety and youth violence prevention.

The International Association of Chiefs of Police
515 North Washington Street, Alexandria, VA 22314
(703) 836-6767

Founded in 1983, the International Association of Chiefs of Police (IACP) is the world's oldest and largest nonprofit membership organization of police executives, with over 20,000 members in over 100 different countries. The IACP's leadership consists of the operating chief executives of international, federal, state, and local agencies of all sizes. The IACP publishes *Police Chief Magazine*.

National Association of Police Organizations
317 South Patrick Street, Alexandria, Virginia   22314
(703) 549-0775
e-mail: infor@napo.org

The National Association of Police Organizations (NAPO) is a coalition of police unions and associations from across the United States that serves to advance the interests of America's law enforcement officers. NAPO represents more than 2,000 police units and associations, 241,000 sworn law enforcement officers, 11,000 retired officers, and more than 100,000 citizens who share a common dedication to fair and effective crime control and law enforcement.

National Criminal Justice Association (NCJA)
720 Seventh Street NW, Washington, DC   20001
(202) 628-8550 • fax: (202) 448-1723
e-mail: info@ncja.org
website: www.ncja.org

The NCJA is an association of state and local police chiefs, judges, attorneys, and other criminal justice officials that seeks to improve the administration of state criminal and juvenile justice programs. It publishes the monthly newsletter *Justice Bulletin*.

US Department of Justice, Office of Justice Programs
810 Seventh Street NW, Washington, DC   20531
website: www.ojp.usdoj.gov

The Department of Justice (DOJ) strives to protect citizens by maintaining effective law enforcement, crime prevention, crime detection, and prosecution and rehabilitation of offenders. Through its Office of Justice Programs, the department operates the National Institute of Justice, the Office of Juvenile Justice and Delinquency Prevention, and the Bureau of Justice Statistics. The Bureau of Justice Statistics provides research on crime and criminal justice. The offices of the DOJ publish a variety of crime-related documents on their respective websites.

Bibliography

Books

| Jeff Cooper | *Principles of Personal Defense.* Boulder, CO: Paladin Press, 2006. |

| Neil Davidson | *'Non-Lethal' Weapons.* New York: Palgrave Macmillan, 2009. |

| Theresa G. DiMaio and Vincent J.M. DiMaio | *Excited Delirium Syndrome: Cause of Death and Prevention.* Boca Raton, FL: CRC, 2006. |

| Jim Fisher | *SWAT Madness and the Militarization of the American Police: A National Dilemma.* Santa Barbara, CA: Praeger, 2010. |

| Gila Hayes | *Personal Defense for Women: Practical Advice for Self Protection.* Iola, WI: Gun Digest, 2009. |

| Lawrence A. Kane, Kris Wilder, and John R. Finch | *The Little Black Book of Violence: What Every Young Man Needs to Know About Fighting.* Wolfeboro, NH: YMAA, 2009. |

| David A. Koplow | *Non-Lethal Weapons: The Law and Policy of Revolutionary Technologies for the Military and Law Enforcement.* New York: Cambridge University Press, 2006. |

Mark W. Kroll and Jeffrey D. Ho — *Taser Conducted Electrical Weapons: Physiology, Pathology, and Law.* Minneapolis, MN: Springer, Charles C. Thomas, 2010.

Nick Lewer — *The Future of Non-Lethal Weapons: Technologies, Operations, Ethics, and Law.* New York: Routledge, 2002.

J. Marchington — *Counter-Terrorism Weapons and Equipment.* Dulls, VA: Brasseys, 2003.

Craig Meissner — *Disguised Weapons: The Law Enforcement Guide to Covert Guns, Knives, and Other Weapons.* Boulder, CO: Paladin Press, 2002.

Michael E. Miller — *Police Taser Utilization: The Effects of Policy Change.* El Paso, TX: LFB Scholarly, 2008

Lorna A. Rhodes — *Total Confinement: Madness and Reason in the Maximum Security Prison.* Los Angeles, CA: University of California Press, 2004.

Darrell L. Ross and Ted Chan, editors — *Sudden Deaths in Custody.* Totowa, NJ: Humana, 2006.

Howard E. Williams — *Taser Electronic Control Devices and Sudden In-Custody Death: Separating Evidence from Conjecture.* Springfield, IL: Charles C. Thomas, 2010.

Periodicals and Internet Sources

Tony Cortina	"Ground War: The Defensive-Tactics System of Choice for Law Enforcement Can Help You Be a Better Fighter—Even If You Don't Wear a Badge," *Black Belt*, March 2011.
Nicole Dyer	"The Shock Bullet: A Shotgun Slug Replaces Lead with Electronics to Deliver a Nasty but Non-Lethal Shock," *Popular Science*, April 2010.
The Economist	"Proto-Robo Cop; Taser Diversifies Its Arsenal," January 2, 2010. www.economist.com.
The Economist	"Under Fire; Policing the Mobs," August 13, 2011. www.economist.com.
The Economist	"Zappers for Coppers; Arming the Police," November 29, 2008. www.economist.com.
Extremetech.com	"Cute Little Tasers Spark Controversy," August 15, 2007. www.extremetech.com.
Michael Joseph Gross	"Shock and Ow!" *GQ*, July 2010.
Ashley R. Harris	"Electroshock Therapy," *Newsweek*, December 24, 2007.
Kimriell Kelly	"More Taser Accountability," *Chicago Reader*, May–June 2010.

Paul Rothman   "Even Non-Lethal Weapons Require Good Judgment," *Security Technology Executive*, May 2010.

Joe Russell   "Story of Taser-Like Phone Has Shocking Conclusion," *Los Angeles Business Journal*, November 22, 2010

Sascha Segan   "Taser Stops Your Kids from Sexting," *PC Magazine Online*, January 6, 2010.

R. Thomas   "Shocking Results: Corrections Departments Consider the Benefits of Adding Taser," *Chicago Reader*, May–June 2010.

Trail Daily Times   "Police Too Quick to Use Taser," April 21, 2011. www.traildailytimes .ca.

Patricia Treble   "The Taser Debate, Down Under," *Maclean's*, October 25, 2010.

Kelly Virella   "Taser Timeout," *Chicago Reporter*, May–June 2010.

Lizzie   "Have Gun," *New Yorker*, March 3,
Widdicombe   2008.

Austin Wright   "A Wall of Tasers," *National Defense*, December 2009.

Index